CONVERSATIONS WITH DAVID ❧

In the Beginning

CONVERSATIONS WITH DAVID
Volume I 𝒆

IN THE
BEGINNING

by Jeanette Kandl

HARBINGER HOUSE 𝒆 TUCSON

Harbinger House, Inc.
Tucson, AZ

Library of Congress Cataloging-in-Publication Data

Kandl, Jeanette, 1931–
    Conversations with David / by Jeanette Kandl.
      p.   cm.
    Contents: v. 1. In the beginning.
    ISBN 0-943173-10-8 (pbk. : v. 1) : $7.95
    1. David, King of Israel. 2. Spirit writings. I. Title.
BF1311.D38K36   1988   133.9'3—dc19   88-16517

To my son, Edward, without whom none of this would have happened.

JK

This book is dedicated to the seekers who want to know the truth. We wish to reach the ones who know more about our side of the veil, and more about love, but do not know how to express it. We are trying to keep it informative, truthful, and mind-expanding, for when you read the simple story that is to come, you will wonder why you didn't figure it out for yourself. It is there.

DAVID

CONTENTS ❧

MANY YEARS AGO, Jeanette Kandl attended a meditation meeting sponsored by the Association for Research and Enlightenment. Completely unfamiliar with either metaphysics or meditation, she was quite unnerved by the experience at first. But the results were so positive, she remained with the association for four years.

The leader of the group was a trance medium who channeled an entity called Julian. During one session Jeanette was told, "You are going to be a deep-trance medium." This came as a shock, since Jeanette did not think very highly of her abilities and didn't even "meditate very well."

At a later private session, Julian confirmed that an entity named Lillian would be coming through her. He described Lillian to Jeanette and suggested that she meditate for twenty minutes each night. For the next few weeks, Jeanette did much soul-searching, crying and praying. The magnitude of this new undertaking worried her, and she was concerned about the integrity of channeling.

When her son, Edward, returned home, he offered to help her fulfill Julian's prophecy. Together they would try and ascertain the validity of her channeling. He said, "I don't believe in this, but I'll tell you if it is real and honest."

Each night they sat in meditation. As they began one evening, Jeanette heard a strange noise. She turned to Edward and asked, "What was that?"

"Lillian is trying to come through," he said, "and I know it's real because she is humming in key, which you never did in your life." After that, Edward became Jeanette's main support while she developed her ability. She channeled Lillian for five years before David, the entity who identifies himself as King David of the Israelites, finally spoke. Unlike Lillian, who gave only personal readings, David was a teacher. He held forth on the deepest concerns of humanity, revealing the secrets of existence, death, and eternity.

Jeanette Kandl is indeed a deep-trance medium, achieving a level of intensity similar to that which Edgar Cayce experienced when he channeled his information. She has no recall of the information she channels, until she hears the tapes or reads the transcripts.

This book evolved over a period of almost ten years. During that time, the original group of five changed to include all the following people:

B.E., a Ph.D. who teaches English literature at a New England university;

Marcie, a professional artist;

Joyce, an executive secretary in a large corporation;

Bill, the owner of a plumbing company;

S.P., a Ph.D. in physics with an electronics firm;

Edward, Jeanette's son, an electrical technician;

Lynn, an executive secretary;

Betty, a public relations executive;

Lucille, a teacher of metaphysics;

Naomi, the transcriber of David's tapes.

Although Jeanette was initially skeptical of the radical information Lillian and David communicated, she has come to appreciate the wisdom of their knowledge.

In 1978 Jeanette was ordained as a minister in the Church of Ageless Wisdom, an interdenominational church based in Philadelphia. At one time she had a congregation and conducted services regularly. Because of her physical disabilities, she regretfully had to discontinue these.

The book which follows here is the first volume of a large body of material transcribed directly from the recordings of David's sessions. The transcribed manuscript was edited by the publishers to eliminate the unnecessary repetitions so often found in oral documents and to correct David's errors in the grammatical and literary construction of English. Neither the information nor the method of presentation has been altered.

David reveals himself here as an extraordinary personality: charming, self-critical, and highly intelligent. The message is more extraordinary still, carrying tremendous ramifications in all phases of human concern—be they personal, theological, ecological, sociological, medical, or astrophysical.

Fr. Gary Yamamoto

CONVERSATIONS WITH DAVID ❧

In the Beginning

T HIS IS DAVID. I am not used to being in a body. It is difficult for me to get used to, especially since I am coming as a male entity into a female body. That does quite a bit to your identity, you know, feeling smoothness and no beard. When I was David, I had a beard, and it is hard to assimilate the fact that I am coming through a female body. Not that I am upset with it. It's going to take a while to get used to using the body and moving the hands.

The fear that I have in being in her body is the premortal fear of being stuck and not being allowed out. This fear comes from the beginning when we came down and entwined ourselves in animal bodies, and so enjoyed the fact that we forgot how to get out. It is the fall that the Bible calls the first sin, the Original Sin. It is becoming involved and not being able to get out. This will not happen to me, but in the beginning the fear is there. It is the fear you have before you go to sleep at night; sometimes you feel you are falling and you wake up with a start. It is the fear you have when you are locked in a room and cannot get out, a claustrophobic fear.

This was the first fear, and this is the fear that now is going to make me back out until I am used to the idea of being with her. She had this fear in the beginning also, that she would leave and one of us would stay and not remember how to get out. This will not happen, but it is an innate fear in every soul when it inhabits something that is not its own true body. We must overcome the fear of entrapment. There are also our vibrations of the spirit on our side of the veil. We are much quicker. I have to slow down my vibrations and not harm her in doing so. So the fear is, are we harming her, are we taking too much of her life force away from her? Will she decide not to come back, and entrap us? Does she want possession so badly that she will possess me and not let me go, which sometimes can happen? But yet, if it does happen, it is written. When a baby is born and it is written that he is to have a soul and a spirit, there is still the fear of entrapment, even though it is his or her free will.

Q: Even though they want the earth life, they still feel it?

David: Yes, of course, because as much as I wish to speak through the medium, the basic fear is still there the first time, even the second time. Now it is not there, you see. Now I know it is an in-and-out, but the first time coming through it is creation all over again. It is entrapment all over again. It is the one basic fear.

Q: If Jeanette's body were to get extremely frightened while you were in it, could you possibly get trapped?

D: No, no, but we would have a few bumps going in and out. [Laughter.] It is her body and she is allowed to protect it, but it would do a little bit to both our nervous systems, because she would rush right back in. It has happened. It would not kill her, but it would take a while to settle down.

Q: Do you have to get out before there's room for her to get back in?

D: Yes, we do not often do it together. If she is here, I sometimes can come in and join her. But when she completely empties out of her body, so that I am in complete command of the body, it is better for her. During that time I am in essence trapped, for I have taken over complete control of the body and she has gone elsewhere. I am trapped, not by the idea that I cannot get out, but with the responsibility of caring and watching out for her body and not overtaxing it.

Q: When she's having pain with her back, can you feel this pain yourself while you're in her body?

D: When she has been having pain in her back and I am in her body, she has no pain in her back. We could cure her back. This is not a problem, but she will not learn her lesson if we do this. She must learn never to allow her body to get into this state of disuse. She has not listened to us. She will probably be riding that bike until she is a hundred and three, but it is not important. We could cure anyone, but that does not teach them what they wish to know. We cannot take their lessons away from them, or they will have them back again, and worse. Each one must find their own answer.

Q: Are you speaking through any other medium while working with us on this material?

D: No. This is the only material coming through. I would not do that to you.

Q: We wondered if you would tell us something about yourself. Have you incarnated since appearing as David, the King of the Israelites?

D: Yes, not always as a king. I had to learn to be a beggar. I had to learn to be a blind man and I had to learn to be a prostitute, because though I was a great man, I thought I was great, and greatness is not to go to your head. These were things that I chose, that I needed to learn. Will I come back again as a great man or a great woman? I do not know, for the responsibilities of being a great person are many and it is harder on the spirit to be a great person, to be revered and not allow it to go to your head. It takes much coming back to get used to just being what you truly are, one with God. No one is better, no one worse. All are just God's children, on the same level with each other. To come back as a great spirit again is something I will give much thought to, for it is better for the spirit to be one of the lowly ones: you learn more deeply and easily than you do as someone who is revered and adored.

Q: Were you great at the time you slew Goliath in the story of David and Goliath in the Bible?

D: I was always great. [Laughter.] Oh yes, I was great, of course.

Q: Were you just in tune with God at the time you slew Goliath?

D: Everyone is in tune with God. All you have to do is know it. The king was in tune. The generals were in tune to allow me to go and do it, for truly, I knew I could do it. But I was frightened, extremely frightened. I used much bravado going down there, but my legs shook and I said, "God, if you ever help me, help me now. If this is what you wish, help me now. If this is truly a message from you and not just my arrogance, help me now." He helped me. But at other times when I thought I was in tune, it was just my arrogance and not being in tune. It is difficult to know on earth whether you are in tune or you are arrogant.

Q: How do you know the difference?

D: You don't. You just do a lot of praying. Do the best you can and listen to what your enemies say of you. Your friends will always say you're great and then whisper behind your back about how great you're not. But your enemies will lay it on the line. Listen to them. Not many do. Your friends will protect you. Is there something else?

Q: Your psalms were beautiful.

D: Yes, weren't they. [Laughter.] But they were also inspired writing, and most came from my heart. God helped me with the words. In the original they are even more beautiful than the translations. The English language does not have the beauty in it that the Hebrew and the Aramaic do. They didn't do such a bad job, but the original is much, much better.

Q: Are we protected on these roads that are icy and slippery?

D: You must do your own protecting on the roads.

Q: I just wondered if anyone else is with us?

D: You know it is easy to depend on God to do everything. But God does not do everything. If you go along and have a bad carburetor or bad hoses or bad tires, you cannot say, "Dear God, you know next week I'll fix it." Everything has an age when it must go, and if it is your hose, perhaps we can hold it together for an hour or two longer. But what happens to the human being when we allow that to happen?

Q: We're not developing the power of our own mind?

D: No. You will think: Well, it held together for two weeks now, it will hold together for two more weeks. You won't get it fixed. When it breaks, usually in the middle of the road, you get upset. Do you see what I am saying? This depending on God and your mind power to hold something together that you know needs to be fixed is not good, unless it is an emergency. Get me to the next gas station or to where it can be fixed—yes, but not through a year. You usually wait until it breaks down to have it fixed, therefore there is a lesson in that. The truckers and pilots always check their instruments before they go, for they know that those instruments hold their lives in their hands. And if they are stupid enough to drive on faulty instruments, God cannot protect them from their own stupidity.

&

Our book is to be the answer to all questions. If someone reads this book and comes up with a question about it, then we have failed. I wish this book to be *the answer*. Not anyone else's answers, just mine. I want this book to be read so that there are no questions that need to be asked. This is why I have asked you people to be with me, for I am still a bit imperial. I am learning, in this lifetime that I am coming through, in your lifetime also. When I was a king I could not be questioned. I need to be questioned this time. So please question me. And all questions are important.

Is there a stick or something? I wish to hold something. I am used to my stick.

Q: Just don't hurt yourself.

D: No, I'm used to it. [Laughter.] I have always had a stick or a staff, or my slingshot. I always had something heavier in my hand to hold.

Q: We met with Lillian [another entity channeling

through Jeanette Kandl] this week, and we asked her what the relationship was between the five of us, the instrument, and yourself. She said we better ask you.

D: Let me put it this way. We have all been together many times, not often as this complete group.

We need input from everyone in this book. This is a book for children to read. It is a book that needs explanations. There is a reason each of you will get different ideas of what should be put down. It is important that you do. We need all five concepts. All five ways of looking at it, for it is not a book for one person to read. It is a book for many people to read. We need five concepts at least. We wish all ideas on it. There will be changes, as always in a book. They are my words, but I am not hurt by what people do with them. Egos are not to be involved in this at all. Only each one helping and working to improve the book until it is satisfactory. No one of you has the only answer. So egos are not to be there, changes are to be many. I am not done dictating yet, the book is nowhere near completion.

But it must be started now, for the lessons of learning to meld together and work together as a group, instead of five separate people, are what you have asked us to help you learn. We are helping you form a group that is interested not in *I* the individual, but *we* the group. By the time this is over, individuals in the group will not matter. It will be the group as a whole, for that is where you will build your energies up and get your energies from. There will be a companionship, a closeness that will not ever be replaced. It will be a feeling of oneness, and when you are off to your different parts of the world, that feeling of oneness will still be there. You will still be able to draw on each other and give to each other. When you start letting go of the ego and working for the good of all (this is the lesson working on this book is teaching you), you forget the "I" and work for the good of all. When you can do it for a small thing like a book, you can start doing it for a big thing like the world. *I*, the ego, must be submerged to *we*, the world. These are the lessons you requested before you came onto this earth, and this is what we are trying to help you learn. If you learn, if you do not learn, it is not for us to say. It is for you to say. If you do not learn, we do not feel we have failed or you have failed, for always the seed is there. It may be that when the group is finally dispersed, you will not feel oneness with each other, but the seed of oneness has been planted.

It will go on and grow until eventually you do feel the oneness. This is what earth is, the oneness of all with one and all with all, with God, and with the other people of God, for you are within God. All together you create God. You are within God. You are part of God. You are not separate entities from God or from each other. You are all one. The only thing on earth that makes you different is being locked up in a body. Your spirit is not one, for each of you have many spirits with you, and many of your spirits visit, and are friends, and are one. They know the concept of oneness. In oneness the ego, the I, is left out and it is "we are." Jesus himself, who had the Christ Spirit, had his apostles and they had their disciples, for they were one and the ego was forgotten, or should have been. The oneness of all is the feeling that you asked to learn, or to have the opportunity to start to learn. Here in this small humble room, the oneness seed is being planted. Each one will not grow at the same rate. They are not planned to grow at the same rate, but are planted in the same fertile soil to grow at their own speed.

All of you will be guided on how the book should be. All of you will hear your guides, or I, or Lillian telling you this or that, and when it is finally completed, you will see that it will meld beautifully into one. All the changes, all the corrections, all the steps needed, all the things that all of you do will create this book, and that is how we will put the power in the book, even more than the words that are in there. The power of love, of oneness, of joy, of helping each other, of losing the ego, of just concentrating on this book helping mankind is how you will help yourselves. And from this will grow greater things.

From what you see here, how you see it work, you will find that the ego will not be so huge. It will be in proportion, it will be how it should be. Definitely the ego should be there, but not huge. Your ego must bow to another's ego and say we are equal. For truly you are equal with the animals, with idiots, with drunks. Your egos are spirit and they are all equal. Their bodies may be different, their intelligence on earth may be different, but they are equal in the eyes of God, and they are equal in the eyes of each other's spirits. No one is above or below the other. All are equal, all have good input, all are loved.

What we have given you here in gentle English are the stories of the mysteries that you will find if you look through all the scriptures, all the tarots, all the hidden books of all the religions. We have broken them down into clear English. They can be found. They run parallel to these other mysteries. These are the truths, from the beginning to now, or until this race here, this fifth race of man. We hope we have managed to explain the beginning of our souls and our spirits, until now. We hope we have given you something to live by, and we hope that it rings a bell with the many who are initiates and don't even know it. The many who feel they are untutored, unschooled, but who are geniuses in their hearts, who are truly the intelligent ones when it comes to the things that are known, but not known. This is our small, simple story. We may not have answered every question in the world, but we have answered enough so that you do not have to ask too many more. We hope that this has set you wondering about the future, looking and seeking more. We hope it has answered the questions that your heart did not know it was asking.

We have done our humblest. We have tried to explain, to clear up the mysteries. Jesus tried, Buddha tried, Confucius tried, everyone tried. We tried to make them no longer mysteries, but to bring them to the common people, to all who should have it, and take it out of the hands of the priests or the intelligentsia.

For those of you who get nothing from this book, I suggest that you put it aside and pick it up again in a few years, when you are ready. Those of you who accept it and go on a spiritual high with it, I suggest that you meditate and pray and realize that the high is within yourself. Do not try to force it on anyone else. The experiences you get from this book are personal. No one else will have a like experience. Do not try to force them to have it. Each experiences differently. Each experiences God where they are, and where they are at. Do not feel badly if you do not have an "enlightenment." Do not feel that you are not on the spiritual path if you do not feel an enlightenment over anything that you hear or say.

Follow merely the still small voice within you that says, "I know I am a part of God. My search may not be over, but perhaps I have started the journey with one step." This book may be the first step, it may be the middle step, but it is a step toward learning, toward growing. Each one accepts it in his own way. If you have criticism of it, that is fine. We expect to be criticized. If you enjoy it, that is also fine, for we know some will enjoy it. If we have teased your minds to go further, then we indeed have accomplished what we have come for. If in answering every question we have raised other questions, read it over again, and you will see that it is answered in there somewhere. This is a book to be read with the mind, but also with the heart and with the spirit. It is a book that we give to you from this side, with our love and blessing, and with the spirit. We hope you handle it gently. And that you will handle each person, and each thing, and each part of this universe with gentleness and with love. For the creed we have preached here is love.

CHAPTER ONE

The First World: Creation

I WILL BE TEACHING things that are not being taught now. I will teach the feelings of humans and the feelings of our side of the veil, and the differences. I will teach you the half-life, so to speak, of living both on our side of the veil as we do, and on your side of the veil. I will be teaching the importance of when you are not meditating and not on our side of the veil; the importance of everyday living, which most people who are into the physical tend to think is not important. It is easier not to face the reality of everyday living. I will teach you to meld the two so that you are neither so earth-bound, nor so bound to our side. The worlds will come together.

I would like you to sit back, be quiet, let your mind go blank, and make believe that this is the beginning of creation. You have just been created. You know no joy, no sorrow, nothing. Everything is in balance. Perfect. You are perfect. You are whole. You have no need to know anything. You just are.

Then you watch creation: the worlds, the earths, the planets. It is similar to watching a television show with the sound off, or one where you hear noise, but it is in another language. You have no idea what is going on. It is all neither confusing nor interesting. You are just watching it, for it is creation. Then suddenly you notice this planet called Earth and you look down and say, "Oh, that's interesting. Let us go and examine it."

Now, before you go, these little spirits, these little bitty souls, the fairies, the animals, the birds, the tree spirits are all saying, "Ooo, that was created for us. We feel as if it is home. May we go down? May we visit this planet?"

And of course God says, "It is created for the animals. It is created for the trees. Yes, you spirits may go down." You watch these spirits hurrying and scurrying, for they have great joy and they have laughter. They go down and enter into the trees that up until this time had no particular life in them, only the body forces. Nothing had its own personality. The tree spirits went into the trees, and the little ones decided they would be birds. The big ponderous ones decided they would visit for awhile in the dinosaur bodies. Now they were not entrapped in these bodies. They could go back and forth and change as they wished.

You watch this and you see they are having fun. It looks interesting. Your curiosity is aroused and you think "Oh, I would like to visit there, go in and out like they're doing, and choose which bodies or which things to be. What makes them appear so content? Let us go and visit along with their spirits."

You ask permission, and God agrees. I'm making this quite simplified now.

So you go down. You do what they are doing. You discover joy. You are eating. You are enjoying the food. You think this is great fun, until suddenly the animal spirit you are with gets frightened. There is something coming after this animal. It frightens the spirit. You are not sure you want to be frightened, so you leave and find another body to go into, perhaps a tree. A tree looks interesting; it sits there and it watches. So you go along with the tree spirit for awhile. It is enjoyable, sometimes a little dull. You are doing this for years, centuries perhaps, going from one to another.

Finally you go into another animal body. You are there eating, and suddenly some other animal comes to attack. Now you want to get out. You are frightened because you are going to lose the ability to get out. It blocks out everything else. You are trapped. Now the terrible fear of being trapped comes. It holds you in there, you cannot run. You are not the spirit that is making this. You are not the brain. You are more intelligent than the brain that is there. You are saying to the spirit, "Run, do something! Let's get away! Let me free!" And the spirit says, "You are free. It is I who am trapped." You are free to go, but you cannot because of the fear. This animal is coming to attack you, to hurt you. You pick up the fear from the spirit that you are with, for they have lived through this before. You are terribly frightened in that moment, and that one moment is the moment you forgot how to get out. Fear is the only thing that keeps you entrapped now.

You have seen children a few days old suddenly cry for no reason. They wake up and realize they are trapped in a body and cannot get out. This is the protest of the fall. You get used to it after awhile and accept it, but the memory of the baby is still entwined with our side where we could move and talk. It is very frustrating for a high spirit to find itself trapped in a small body where it cannot communicate. It must learn to do it all over. Slowly through the years this memory is forgotten, but in some babies the frustration is there until they can start walking.

Now you may say I'm being redundant, but I want to impress upon you that this is the first fear, the first feeling of man on earth. The feeling of being trapped. Even today it is the worst feeling you can have. Being trapped by love. Being trapped by circumstances. Being trapped by your body. Being trapped by sickness. It is the feeling of frustration, the fear of not being able to get away.

From there it slowly evolved into the drive for survival. Now you notice joy is not in here yet. Joy and laughter are not here. Survival, you have to eat. You have to find a place to sleep. You have to worry. In the moment you were trapped, you lost the feeling of God being here. You became trapped in everyday material things, and no longer looked skyward or flew from place to place. You no longer looked to God for the answers. You looked to the earth, for you had to survive. You did not like what you were in, but you had to survive. You have a strange feeling in your stomach, and when you eat this grass or another animal, it eases this pain, and truly, hunger is a pain. It is an aching. It is a wishing to be back on our side of the veil. It is the hunger for more than food.

You go looking for food. You get tired. You have never been tired before. You're suddenly very tired. You're looking for a place to sleep, and the spirit that is with you, the animal spirit says to you, "You cannot direct me where to go. I am an animal. I have been an animal. I wish to be an animal. You do not know what you wish to be. You are coming along with me for the ride, but you are not an animal. You are here with my spirit, but you are not me. You will be here with me until I am no longer here." So he marches, and you are tired. You are frightened. You're alone. All you have is the animal spirit who will not listen to what you say. For he truly knows the world of survival. He has been there before. You have only popped in and out and played games. Can you feel the fear that is in you? The wanting to go, the wanting to escape, wanting to be free, but forgetting all the time to look up, for you are now looking down. You are now bound by material things. If the fear had gone, you could have remembered how to get out, but it did not go.

You are frustrated. You cannot get out. You have anger and the starting of the feeling of inferiority and the mate superiority. The animal is making you feel inferior, but you feel superior. You tell yourself that some day when you are no longer in this body, you will make this animal do your will, for surely you are not inferior. The animal spirit says, "Ho-hum, if you're so superior, why don't you have your own body? Why are you trapped in my body? Why can you not get out? *I* have chosen to come into this body. *I* like this body. *I* am not afraid of it. *I* am peaceful. *I* enjoy being on earth. You are borrowing mine."

At times you may get the feeling of someone else possessing you, because you, at one time, possessed somebody else's body. An animal, yes. But notice that animals are content being animals. There is not one of them who wishes to be anything but what they are. It is humans who wish to be more, who wish to be better, who wish to be superior, and who even at times wish to be inferior. So we go on for generations.

Now the others are watching from their side and they are saying, "Listen to us. You can get out." But you are not hearing anymore. You cannot hear the gentle voices because of the fear, because of the wanting to survive. You are panicky. You are listening to no one. You are alone for the first time. You have made your first step on the earth plane. You are stuck and frightened.

When you die, you go up to the other side. The more you come back, the more you die, the farther away you feel from those of us who have not been on earth. We say to you, "You know that you are back here. You do not have to go down there again." You say, "What do you know? Don't talk about it until you have tried it. We are trapped." We say, "You are not trapped. You are free now. You have died. You are reborn on our side. You do not have to go back." And you say, "Yes, we do, for now we smell, we feel, we taste. We are trapped. We are addicted to the feeling of earth, to the feeling of being there."

The spirits who are in the trees are frightened too. They are afraid to make any movements for fear someone will come and attack them, as the animals are attacking each other for food. So they stay where they are. They forget how to get out. They watch and they wait. Then they see a storm come up, it is fire, there is electricity, they are burning. They are so frightened they cannot escape and they die. And when they die they find they are back on our side of veil, but still not able to communicate, for they have discovered fear, which we on this side do not know about. They discovered fright survival, which we do not know about.

We were balanced. We could not understand why they were fearful, why they thought they could not get back. Why they were concerned with survival, and why they thought they had to go back on earth again. But they were trapped in a cycle of leaving God and being on earth. On the other side the spirits do not understand why they must go back and do it again.

They are highly embroiled in this situation. We look from our side. We hear the tears, the confusion, the possession, the superiority, the anger, the greed. We don't see any joy. If you have noticed, I have said the spirits have taken over *only* the trees and the animals. The only true joy in the world was with the birds. No one wished to take over the birds. They were the only joy in the world, and no one listened.

We watched from our side and said, "Now they must be helped. We must bring joy to them. We must bring another type of body down there that they can get into and enjoy, one that better matches their spirit. We cannot have them with more than their two feet on the ground, because with two arms on the ground, they are forgetting to look up. They're forgetting to look at the birds. They are forgetting to look at God. They are forgetting where they came from. They are becoming very entwined in earth matters just being stuck down there."

We decided to create a body for the spirit to go into. We looked over all the animal bodies on earth at that time, and the one closest to what we wanted was, of course, what they call the missing link. The apes were inquisitive, joyful, but too cumbersome. They plod and are slow moving. If we are coming down as an alien group from another world, so to speak, we have to be able to run, to get away from animals that will think of us as food or something curious to look at and step on, because the animals have always been curious. Their curiosity brought them here. So we decided to create a good body, able to move around, and with hair for protection to keep the soft spots warm; covering the head, under the arms, in the private sections, and perhaps even on the legs. Some of them will not be in places where they will need covering. We must put these bodies all over where there are animals who have spirits from outside attached to them, not the animal spirits who are content to be animal spirits.

In the Book of Genesis it says, "And they were covered with hair and skin, and they were put down on earth." We, the ones who wished to bring love and joy, will inherit these bodies and slowly show the ones who are in the animals how to get out of their bodies and come and join us. Of course, we will not forget how to get back again. We can hop in and out. Oh, such big plans we had. But we did not realize earth was such a fascinating place to be. So many different things. So was created man and woman. Men and women, each of their kind in each of the sections of the world. How many in each section, suddenly awakening? Tribes, ten-twenty here, ten-twenty there, ten-twenty over there. Friendly, nice people. You would have liked them. They enjoyed earth. The animals frightened them, but there was peace and joy. They loved. They were the opposite of fear.

They say the opposite of love is hate. That is nonsense. The opposite of love is fear. There are two emotions only: one is fear, one is love. Like the primary colors, from the blending and melding of them come all other emotions. Think that one over, for it is true.

&

Q: Specifically what do you mean by Original Sin? Do you mean the actual entrapment as being Original Sin, or the enjoyment of the feelings that led to the entrapment?

D: Original Sin in the Bible is described as the Fall of Man, but it was not sex. It was entrapment. It was when the souls got down to earth and forgot in their enjoyment, or in their first fear of being attacked, how to get out. The Bible calls it the Original Sin. They had to figure out some reason for people being on earth, for being thrown out of heaven, so to speak. They called it the Garden of Eden, which of course was our side of the veil. The Original Sin was supposedly with the serpent, which is an animal, or the Kundalini knowledge, the tree of knowledge. There is much symbolism. For men have tried to think how man could have left our side of the veil and gone down to suffer on earth. Moses decided to call it sin because everyone on earth was suffering, as if you only suffer for your sins, but that is not true.

Q: You said the people who came down to inherit bodies were more than two, not just Adam and Eve. Did Adam and Eve really exist, the way we understand it?

D: Let me put it this way. Just as the animals on earth did not just start with only two, people did not start with only two. No woman could have enough children to populate this world. There were many that came, that were symbolized in the Bible as Adam and Eve. Mother and Father the starters, you see, but we will get into that.

ॐ

The beginning of the earth was simple, because God is simple. No one has asked how God created earth, or how God created animals. To prove the human ego, the concern of most people is how Adam and Eve were created.

It is easy to accept that earth was just created. It is easy to accept that animals were created. Go back to any of your books on the creation of animals and they will say protozoa, amoeba, from the swamp, from the water, crawled up. Who created the first one that was there? Were there two? Were there many? I will say this: earth did not start from a seed. The hen came before the egg, and life did not crawl from the ooze, life of animal or man. They were created much as this house was created. It was a thought of God. He planned it out, and with his hands, so to speak, put it together. This house could not have been created without thought. Thought is the creator of everything. If you used your mind properly, you could think that that picture or that mirror could move, and it would move because you have thought of it.

There are things called apports, that appear from nowhere, but they have been thought of and they appear. That is how the earth was. It was thought of: it appeared. This is how the animals were. They were thought of and appeared, and so too with man. Thought of and appeared.

The body is a gift from God. If you do not take care of the body, you cannot help other people, nor can you help yourselves. When you get into your body, you have to first learn to live with the body before you can bring peace and joy to anyone else.

Look at your body this week as if you have never had a body before, and you just now entered into this amazing body that was thought up. Look at it. See that the fingernails grow. A body that sloughs off many diseases, if you wish it to. A body that is a well equipped machine, perfectly running. A body that no one except God could invent.

We are down on earth, picking fruit from the trees. We find that the earth is not always a friendly planet to be on. Some of the plants we tried to eat are poisonous and kill us, and we have pain. That is a terrible thing. We have never felt pain before, and we did not want to die. This was the first death. This was the first not wanting to go, for truly we were just born. We wanted to stay and do things. Then we learned to do things with love and joy, but to also be extremely careful, because everything is not friendly. Now starts suspicion. You look at your neighbor, and find out that your neighbor has eaten the same thing and has not died. You wonder why, and it frightens you a little bit for it is the unknown.

So you had to learn, rather than trying to help these people who are stuck in the animals. Some are enjoying it, some are not. They still have the fear. They are forgetting now to look up, but we are the crusaders. We are going to help them, but first we must help ourselves get used to our own bodies.

Therefore, we get entwined again. This is not fear this time. We did this willingly, but now we worry whether we have enough innate intelligence to take care of the body on earth. I know how to take care of my spirit on this side of the veil. But I have a body to take care of. What can it do? What can it not do? The full answers of how to take care of it were not created with it. They say now that back in the old days, the bodies were superior. Food was better. They were not poisoning themselves. The air was better. That was not so. With all this time around, their body was not superior. The body was exactly the same as it is today. There were perhaps not as many diseases in as many places as there are today, but each one of the diseases were in their own place.

People say cavemen were the first men. No, cavemen were the simple ones, the ones who went back to the land. There was always great intelligence, *always* great intelligence. For the spirit was born balanced from creation. The spirit did not have to grow. The spirit was intelligence inheriting the body.

The cavemen had a great time doing things. It was interesting. Life was simple. And there was fire long before they thought there was fire. For we had to keep warm. You say, how can cavemen live alongside of people who are intelligent, who are perhaps highly civilized? But you see it now in Australia, with the Bushmen. They live right alongside of the white people and the black people who are of a so-called higher intelligence—who are superior, cultured. But when it comes down to it, who survives best in Australia? The Bushmen, when they're out in their bush country. They have the highest intelligence. For they are gentle people who go along with the earth, much as the cavemen.

The body has not changed. You will see the anthropologist who takes the bones of the Peking man and makes him look like his idea of what the caveman should be. But what would prevent this same anthropologist from using the same bones and using a model of a man today? You would find if he did that, that this man could pass in a crowd and no one would know that he was the Peking man. They used to burn the bodies back then, except those of some who were killed, or some of the mentally lowly, weakhearted people who would run off into the woods, so to speak, and perhaps get hurt. Some of these they are digging up now, and are saying, "This is what man was like." From one bone you cannot say this is what a race was like. What you can merely say is that this is what this man *might* have looked like.

In the preaching of everyday people, they say that in God there is perfection, therefore there can be no sickness. I do not wish to say that is hogwash. The body was given to you, or you created the body. There is no sickness in your spirit. You, the spirit, are perfect, but the body leaves a lot to be desired. In truth, there *is* sickness, disease, and aging. In the beginning, when you were first in bodies, there was also sickness, broken legs, poisons. Though the spirit was perfect, the earth that you chose to live on was not perfect. There is not true harmony on earth, ecologically speaking or naturalistically speaking. But the harmony of nature that everyone speaks of as being so perfect, so easily understood, so in tune that everything is fine, is again hogwash. Earth is a dog-eat-dog world, so to speak.

Animals are not afraid of getting sick, because they have no time sense. A day means nothing to an animal. It gets dark. It gets light. They're content being animals. They are content with just living and praising God in their own way. They do not ever wish to be people. They enjoy being animals. They do not know what sickness is. They think only perfect thoughts, but in truth they get sick, do they not?

They die, do they not? They do not know how to heal. They curl up, they go to sleep, and either they get well or they die. The body gets sick. The soul does not. The spirit does not.

I am saying this because it is extremely important. You must recognize the fact that the body does get sick so you can start making it better. If you ignore the fact and do nothing to make it get better, you are in big trouble.

Faith healing is very good. It works, yes. But the body is not made to last forever. In the beginning, the body was made to last for maybe four or five hundred years. I am talking about the beginning when you first came into your body, because four or five hundred years was nothing, you had no concept of time. It took longer to get sick. It took longer to die. There were not many people on earth.

When you came into your body and walked around with it, you felt your fingernails grow, your hair grow, you had to eat. You had to worry about cleanliness, and untangling your hair so bugs did not get into it.

At the same time, you could also do astral travel. You could leave your body. Now, in the beginning when you did this, the body died for it had nothing to keep it going. You would have to create another body or go into another body. The system was not working out. The soul came into existence so that when you astral traveled, the life forces would still be maintained. The soul's main purpose was to keep the body alive, to work with the body, keep the heart beating, to take care of the hunger that sometimes you did not notice because you were not completely attached to the earth plane. Some of the people, in the beginning, starved to death because they did not know what hunger was. So into creation came the soul. The soul's main purpose was to say to the spirit: I need to wash, I need to love, I need. The soul's main purpose is to say, I need. The spirit's main purpose is to say, I do.

Now you have three things involved in one creation: the body, the soul, the spirit. The blessed trinity that the churches speak of is nothing but the body, the soul, the spirit. The blessed trinity is within you.

Already your high spirits, your love, your humanity are lessened a little, because you have to worry first about your body. You have to worry about getting used to it and caring for it. You have to worry about the soul taking over and directing you when you do not wish to eat, saying, "I am hungry, you better eat." You get involved in living, involved in surviving, involved in giving credence and love to God.

It takes you quite a while to remember that you came down here with a purpose, to help the other souls who are trapped in the animal bodies to get out. We came down with very good intentions, but how are we going to do it? We planned a body, we planned intricate workmanship. We planned that we could walk, we could run, we could escape, we could enjoy, we could make love. But we did not have a plan for getting them out of the animal bodies. The more intelligent ones got together and said, "We came down here with a plan." Now this was about four hundred years into living that someone finally remembered. "We have to start doing something to help our friends who are still trapped, who still are in the cycle of dying and coming back as a tree or a plant. We are living four hundred years, how long is the body going to live? We are going to have to be able to die, go back and tell them on the other side. For now we are on earth and they are not going to say that we do not know what we are talking about."

The next time you incarnate, you must incarnate back into a human body. So you procreate, and after five, six, seven hundred years, finally you die; except for the ones who have had accidents and sicknesses, who went suddenly, not wishing to go because the others haven't. They have gone to the other side and come back as babies. When you die, you go back and you see the ones who have been in the tree bodies and in the animal bodies and you say to them, "See, you do not have to go back again. You have not fallen. This time now, if you do wish to go back, go back in a human body."

The ones who were in the animal bodies and the tree bodies looked at them and said, "But you too are trapped. You too are in a cycle. You too are talking about going back. You too are talking about re-incarnation. Why do *you* not stay here? Why do you wish to go back to the earth also?" The ones who were in the human bodies said, "Because we think the ones who are still here do not know or understand as much as we do. We have forgotten much. We must go back and learn more. We have lost the perfect balance and we must try to find it. We have lost the way back. We are trapped too." And the ones in the animal bodies said to them, "How can we, who are used to being in animal bodies, go into human bodies without acting like animals? There must be a way for us to grow from animal bodies into human bodies on the earth plane, to evolve, and you in your intelligence must help us do this."

The ones with the love and the humanity came down but they did not plan. They rushed in before final plans were made, as many people do today. The animal bodies were still trapping the human spirits, the human spirits with the animal souls and animal spirits. And the ones coming down said to the trapped spirits, "It is not as easy now that we understand what it is like, for we too are trapped. We have great love, but of course we must first worry about our own souls and our own spirits and then help you." There comes the beginning of ego and selfishness.

They lost a little of their humanity and a little of their love, and were interested in their own body and well-being first, and then trying to get the trapped spirits out. This went on, through incarnation after incarnation, through years. This is prerecorded history. This is before the Book of Genesis. This is the first time, the true beginning of earth and the people. There were five endings, so to speak, of the civilizations of the world.

Noah and the ark were not in the first world, they were in the fifth. So I want you to go back before the beginning of the Bible, before the Book of Genesis. You are going back millions of years before this.

We go through building the generations, building up to a beautiful civilization. People helping people. People loving people. People having babies, people caring, gently, a bit of an ego there, yes? They are going on for maybe a thousand years, and suddenly someone says, "We have forgotten our friends. We have lived on the earth plane for two thousand years, and have forgotten our many friends who are still trees and who are still animals, who are still crying in the night for our help." This is the first time remorse sets in, and a feeling of guilt. We have forgotten our purpose.

Then the first Christ Spirit comes down. He was born, so to speak, but the first Christ was not born a man or a woman. He created his body much as the others have done. It was no miracle at that time. You could have children either through sex or just creating.

The Christ Spirit said, "I will show you the way to free our friends. First we must gather them up. We must convince them that they must overrule the spirit of the animal. They have been slaves to the animal and the tree bodies. We must get them to get angry and rebel. We must change their fear to righteous anger. We must convince them that they are as intelligent as the animal body that they are in. They are not slaves to be looked down upon. They must want to be free."

"Do not feel remorseful because you have forgotten them. They are the ones who did not remind you, who were content with their lot. They were pleased with being carried along with their fear and enjoying their fear. We must now make them dissatisfied with what they have, or content enough to stay and be quiet about it. They cannot stay in the animal body and enjoy it, and at the same time tell you that they wish to get out. You cannot help someone unless they are willing to help themselves."

The people said, "This is a very intelligent man. Of course this is what we are supposed to be doing." But the only reason they felt this man, this Christ with the true beautiful spirit, was intelligent, was because he was telling them what they knew and felt inside, but did not give words to themselves. Do you understand what I am saying?

He was their conscience, truly balanced, and made them understand that they could help their brother only if the brother wished to be helped. But he also pricked their conscience, so from that time on, they did not forget about their friends, the animals and trees, but went out and spoke to them as they were. They tried mental telepathy with them, and even got them angry. They said to them, "If you wish to get out, you must help yourselves and we will help you. But you must overcome the master. You must make friends with the animal spirit that you are with, and then divide from it. But do not allow it to be superior to you, or you to be superior to it. Understand it."

It took a lot of preaching. It took a lot of communicating with trees. It took a lot of communicating with spirits. It brought anger. It brought humility. It brought understanding, and in some cases, it brought love—the love of the person who was trapped in the animal body for the animal spirit. Today, the fifth time around, you'll find some people understand animals more than others, because at that time they came to understand.

Now we have covered two thousand years. We have talked about the Christ and the animals.

&

Q: What is God?
D: God is all-knowing, all-powerful, all creation, all creator. It is an intellect, an ever-growing intellect, ever-creating intellect, moving ever forward, that knows everything that is created, that creates everything that is created. God is within everything, is everything, encompasses everything. God is the outer layer of the universe. We are all within God. Not only is God within us, but we are within God. Without us, God could still survive. Without God,

nothing can survive. God knows what is going on. God watches. God is ever creating. He has not stopped creating nor will He ever stop creating, and I do not wish to use "He." Please erase any "he" or "she" because there is no sex. He is above sex, beyond sex. God is completion. God is the beginning, the end, the middle. God is everything, and we are part of the everything that is God. We are part of the ever growing, ever changing, ever creating, ever seeking, ever curious, ever watchful. We are God. The earth is God. The plants, the minerals, the stars, the air, that is all God. God is everything. Is that sufficient answer for you?

Q: Yes. Is God basically a form of energy with manifestations within that energy?

D: Yes.

Q: From and with what substance was the human body created?

D: The human and animal bodies on earth were created with the substance that is still used to make models—clay. The clay was formed into a workable model that life, or the soul, was breathed into, so to speak, to make it flesh. All of the substances of the earth are in the body. It was created as each one felt his or her body should be created, of the different ears, hair, eyes, noses.

There were many models that did not succeed before the spirit went into it, many unworkable models. Finally, they found one where everything worked in tune: the liver, the spleen, the arteries, the brain cells. Now that does not just mean human form. Animal form was the beginning. Most animal forms, if you tear them down, have organs similar to humans. The human body was improved to have the spirit live in it. But it was not made so that it could live on earth easily as the animals were made. It was made merely as the ideal conception of what a human spirit would like to live in.

Q: Were there differences besides color and physical characteristic to the human form? For example, were there several separate evolutionary chains with the best form surviving?

D: There were many sizes, many shapes. There were and still are today, though difficult to find, very little people that you call fairies, brownies, leprechauns, the small ones. You do not see them because they are frightened and hide. They are getting scarcer as the earth is becoming more crowded, but they are living in the deep woods. They are very crafty. There are also pygmies; they were not pretentious enough to feel they should be that much larger than their surroundings. Then there were giants who were seven to twelve feet tall. They no longer exist. The giant bodies were hard to handle. They were not quickly movable and easy to get around. The problem with the smaller bodies was that larger animals could quickly catch them and eat them. So they came to a middle-sized body, which starts about four-two. Six feet was almost a giant. They figured this was the best size for living, to maintain supremacy over the animals and yet be fleet of foot. The giants tired easily. So in that manner, there were trial models for the best bodies, for those that would last the longest and be repaired most easily. For in the beginning, each creator repaired his own creation easily. When it got sick, or had broken arms or legs, the creator was close by. The spirit knew each part of the creation so well that he or she could rearrange the molecules or parts of the body by thinking about it and adjusting them to cure any problem. Today, no one knows that much about their own body to be able to do this. They are trying, but the memory is not that close in most people.

Q: Why were there color differences?

D: We will start from the darkest color on to the lightest color. The black skin does not burn in the sun. The curly hair was an insulation to keep the brain from getting overheated. It was a cooling and warming factor, much as the hair around the pubic area. Every hair around every pubic area is curly for insulation. When it is hot, it sweats so the water of the sweat will cool it.

The Indians in America are, I would not say reddish, but a different brownish color, because it is not as hot as down by the equator. Their hair can be long and straight for the coolness going through it. The yellow [sic] color in the desert country blends mostly with the area they are in, where it is hot during the day and cold during the night. They do not need the deep, deep color. They will not be sunburned, but they need a coloring to keep the infrared light from harming their skin and causing skin cancer. In the Arctic the color is a little lighter. They had to be told to cover themselves. The skin had to be fair so that they would unconsciously know to keep warm, to cover their skin.

As for the size of the ears, in the jungle where it is important to hear things that are nearby, the ears are flat against the skin to hear in all directions. In the deserts, the sounds come from far away so the ears were made larger and more cupped to gather the noise.

Every part of the body was designed where it was created. Now everyone is all mixed up, which is just beautiful. But in the beginning, before they could travel that far from place to place, they had to realize the limitations of the body, of where they were living, and how to protect it. It is very bad in the jungle to put many clothes on. They are doing that now and it is not good. They are getting sick. In the cold countries, it is not good to run around naked, no matter what color you are. But if you are white and you are in a country where it is very hot, you know that you have to cover up, because if you do not, you will burn up. So the white skin means that it must be protected at all times.

&

Q: Please clarify the functions of the spirit and that of the soul.

D: It is something that may have to be taken on faith, but the spirit is you, the you that is reincarnated each time. The same spirit, yes. It is you. It is your superconscious. It is your unconscious. You do not always arrive with the same soul. The soul's main job is to take care of the body. It is also what carries on the genetic features of your mother, your father. It is the memory of the family, and the memory that you are a human being. The spirit, when it comes from another planet, is not always a human being as you are on earth. It is difficult at times to remember that you are a spirit on earth with a human body. The soul tells you and reminds you. You are in a human body, you must eat. The soul says that your grandmother had gray hair at twelve, you will have it at fifteen. The genetics brings the soul. The body is created and ever created, as man and God are creation. Only this time, instead of using the mud, we use parts of the body to make it grow. The food that you eat and parts of your body make it grow, which is an amazing thing. All birth is amazing.

Q: Can it be said that the soul is the conscious mind?

D: Yes, it is the conscious mind but it is also a part of the unconscious. How many times have you seen a child who has never seen his grandmother and you say, "My heavens, he has the same traits as his grandmother." He looks like a Bauers, or he acts like a Weeks, or he acts like a Smith. So it is a combination of the three that you cannot completely separate, except when death comes. Then the soul goes back to have the memory of the spirit washed off, and comes back to take another body, perhaps in another generation of your family. But the spirit may become part of someone else's family. They are two different things that go entirely their own way, for the soul is earth-bound and the spirit is eternity-bound.

Q: When does the soul get the programming it needs for a new reincarnation of some specific spirit?

D: You are going now to the genes, to the memory. It starts in the womb.

Q: Does the soul arrive in a new baby clean and then just pick up the genes and the memories and everything at that time?

D: Yes, it starts as the baby is being formed. There is always a soul with the body. There is not always a spirit with the body. Most of the so-called crib deaths mean that the spirit does not wish to accept that body and will not enter, and the soul can keep the body alive just so long.

Q: Does that mean the spirit didn't enter the body at all in that child?

D: Yes. The spirit can enter the body anywhere

from the time in the womb up until three months after the baby is born.

Q: When you feel life in a baby, that doesn't necessarily mean the spirit has entered?

D: It means the soul is there.

Q: In a coma, does it mean, at times, the spirit leaves?

D: The spirit leaves, but the soul stays.

Q: Yes, the mechanics.

D: Yes. And things are imprinted on the mind. The soul now stays. The spirit astral travels, but it keeps a check on the body. The body is a very important thing when you go on to the other side of the veil, an extremely important thing. For it has been your friend. It has been your temple. It has done your work. You have, in fact, helped create what it is. It is the only true creation you have. When you have left it, you are not sorry, but you stay and make sure that it is taken care of and given some respect. Much like a faithful dog that you love. When it dies, you wish to take care of its body. To put it away, and the memory of it. Often when someone dies, their spirit stays with the body for three or four days, watching what is going to happen. Earthbound spirits who have committed suicide and are running around the earth are usually waiting for someone to find their body and bury it properly.

Q: Could you say that the soul is the spark of life in the body?

D: Yes, and it is dear. It is the recorder of grandfathers. It is the recorder of genes, of your family life. You may create the body, but the soul brings the memory of ancestors back to you. But your spirit lets you know what you are. Sometimes there is rage when you get into your body and find out that you are not what you wanted to be on earth. If you come back female and you truly wish to be male, you feel as if you've been tricked. If you wish to be black and you are white, you feel tricked. And you are sometimes angry with yourself and what you look like, for the soul and the spirit are fighting.

❧

Q: What was the sequence of emotions that led to entrapment? Did fear precede entrapment?

D: Again it is a fine line that we draw here. When we were going in and out of the animal bodies, we would feel a shot of adrenalin or fear and we would see the animal acting strangely. But remember we had no emotions. We watched earth be created with no emotions, for we did not know what was going on. We watched animals kill each other with no emotion, for we had never killed or been killed. The minute the fear would start, we would run out. But one time the spirits got a little lazy. They said, "Let us see what is going on here," because sometimes it looked like a lot of fun. Animals were playing with each other, running back and forth and chasing, what an exciting game that looked like. Some bled a little, but did not know what hurt or pain was. So three or four decided to stay around and watch. We will stay inside. Now, through the thousands of years we've been staying in a little bit longer each time. Stretching the time, oh, another five minutes here will not hurt. Finally, one time when the adrenalin started to run in the animal and fear started, we said, "Let us just stay and watch." Suddenly the terror of the spirit grabs us. The terror of the fighting grabs us, and then the terror that we cannot get out because we have forgotten, we have hung around five minutes too long. We cannot get out. Then even more terror and pain because truly we were with the animal, a part of the animal, feeling its reactions. Feeling pain for the first time is terror. Feeling terror for the first time and the idea of not getting out is again terror, so it was terror upon terror, fear upon fear. A combination of many emotions, but all one. Entrapment and fear and terror.

Q: Did the animals actually experience fear?

D: The animals always had fear. It was an instinct put into them to preserve themselves. But an animal's terror does not last like a human being's terror. An animal can be chased and completely, utterly terrified, run into the woods, and find itself someplace to hide. It watches the terror go by and says, "Oh well," until the next time. They do not remember. It is not a lasting terror. They have no guilt. Why should they be guilty? They eat, they kill one another to eat. Except for your wolverine, some animals just kill to kill.

Q: So in animals we could call this their survival instinct rather than their fear.

D: Yes, that is all it is. We humans have named it terror. A cat who has been chased up a tree by a dog gets up to the top of the tree and knows she's safe. She looks down at the dog and says, "Yep, you missed me that time," and cleans herself and does not worry about it. A human being would get up that tree and sit there and shake and shake all night long, and then get into his house, lock the door, and shake again.

Q: Can we say then that animals have no soul?

D: An animal has a soul. It tells each one that they are a dog or a cat and it brings their instinct to them.

An animal has a spirit, but they did not fall, so to speak. They're not being punished. They choose to come here. They are playing. They have no sense of time.

Q: Do they suffer pain?

D: They suffer pain, but they do not remember it. If a friend of theirs comes over and licks them and says, "Oh, it's all right," they feel better and they can heal themselves. If no one comes and tells them, they can die from the pain, for they are not used to pain. They do not know how to handle it. You cannot talk to them, but they will come back again. They have no desire ever to be a human being, for they have no worries. They like being animals. They like being free. They like enjoying themselves. They have no conscience. A human being tries to give an animal a conscience. We say, "Bad dog," but that dog is doing what is ingrained in him.

They say cats are sneaky. No, cats are not sneaky. Cats move slowly and gently in perfection to catch their food. They are quiet. They are beauty. When you keep them in the house and they do the same stalking, you say sneaky. You give them human feelings. No, they have animal feelings—far superior to human feelings, for they truly trust in God. They truly believe in God. They truly are not afraid of anything, for they know they will go to God. They have not fallen. They don't need a conscience, for they know they do right.

Trees have spirits, much as you, but they have chosen their roles as trees. Feel a tree. Have any of you ever held a tree and felt the energy that is in there, the calmness and healing that are in there? There is a tree spirit in there.

Everything on the earth and in the world is alive.

It is a creation, it had energy, it is a part of the energy of God. Some can express themselves, but men express themselves for just a short time. A tree can outlive a man. A rock can outlive a tree. A mountain and the earth can outlive many, many generations of people and animals. Hold a rock in your hand and feel the energy that is in there. You can receive energy from just a piece of wood in your house. It is no longer attacned to its roots, but it is not into ashes yet. You can still feel it from wood, not perhaps as strong, but it is there. Some people like working with wood because of the energy that comes through it. The remembering of the time that you too were wood or an animal.

ð

Q: What is the source of fear?

D: God created everything. God is all things. There is no evil in this world. There is no devil in this world. Fear came from the human being going inside the animal and not knowing how to get out of it. Man created fear. God knew about it and figured: you created it, now let's see what you're going to do with it. Fear at times is a good thing, and at other times it is a destructive thing. It was created originally for the animals as instinct, to watch out for themselves. So that the lamb would not truly trust the lion, unless the lion was completely full.

It was natural, though, to keep a melded balance of nature for the old and malformed animals to be destroyed gently, so that they would not have to suffer. It was God's way of putting them to sleep permanently. Animals will have to die because that is the natural way of this world. It is a perfect world, where everything evolves or moves or changes or takes care of itself. The waste goes into the ground and forms trees and plants. When something dies, something else will come along and eat what is dead so that it will not rot and smell badly. The animals did not create themselves as man did. God created the animals as he wished, and the soul and spirit took over gladly. Animals could not heal themselves because they did not know what the creation was. When they broke their leg, or were born puny, or could not quite make it, God had other animals who ate them. Balance and gentle death, because in the death pangs the terror was so great that they felt absolutely nothing. They were stiff, the adrenalin went through them and they felt no pain. It is important. The pain was not there. In humans, the pain is.

❧

Q: At death, the soul and spirit separate. Where do the mind and the memories go?

D: With the spirit.

Q: Are all the memories kept?

D: Yes. They are all written on your own record, the Akashic records. It is like a memory bank. When you are on our side, you can go back into your own lives and remember. It is like looking into an album and saying, "Oh yes, there I was at three years old, and there I was at one year, and this was uncle so and so." Total recall of all the past lives is really too bothersome, even for the spirit. It would be like totally recalling every incident that has ever happened to you in your lifetime here on earth. It is easy for us to go to your Akashic records, or to the memory that is implanted on your spirit. It is the same thing.

Q: Why were the spirits created and what is their purpose or function?

D: Why were spirits created? Because God thought about them and so created them. And their function is to be ever creative and ever to grow with God. To ever experience, and ever know. Their function is not to go *back* to God so much as being *one* with God.

Oneness with God means feeling as if you were a part of God and knowing that you are a part of God. Being one with God is being with God, but not returning to the vast energy that is God and just disappearing. For God created you to have your own spirit, and he takes back nothing that he gives. If your child said to you, "Mother, I wish I could go back into the womb again," you would say, "I've created you. That is your problem from here on in. You are you, and I am proud of that fact. I do not want you back. I want you to know that I love you, and you are one with me." This is what God wants, that's all. He doesn't even want it, people want it because of the fall. They feel they have wandered away and they have to find their way back. They are part of God, just as your children are a part of you, no matter where they go or what they do.

You create your own life, and then create and create, and that is what God did. He thought about having friends, so to speak, and the souls and spirits were created. The spirits first, the souls second. All He had to do was think, and it was like an amoeba dividing, and there we were.

&

Q: How did greed enter human beings and animals?

D: In the animal kingdom, it is perfectly balanced.

The people talking about the balance of nature are quite correct, and the only thing imbalancing nature is man. But it was not so much greed as competitiveness, of who could get the most food, and then the larger territory or the most females. It started with the male. When one animal killed another animal, he deserved his full share. Sometimes rather than sharing, he wished to eat the whole thing, and then when he got up whoever wanted the leftovers could come and have some. The others would say, "Oh, he's greedy. He wants it all for himself," and try to attack. In the animal survival kit of memory is the drive to eat all they can today, for they may not find another sick or slow animal for a week, and to survive, they must eat when they can. The mother of the babies says, "I have to get what I can so my babies can survive." Animals do not have a concern about other animals unless they are in trouble. The single-minded purpose of an animal is to enjoy living on earth. To eat the grass and grow, for the grass eaters. For the meat-eating ones, it is to cull the sick and slow ones from the herd. Vultures or carrion-eating animals clean up afterward.

There is never a fear of the predator unless he is out being a predator. If the predator has eaten, the other animals can see that and are relaxed, and they will wander quite close to them and eat. They are only afraid when they sense the vibration from the predator that says, "I am hungry. I am hunting the sick and the slow."

When man was in the animals and learning all of these things, man did not let go of any of these feelings. Man found out that the ones who survived were the ones who were greedy. So greed came into human beings, and greed means that if *I* get the most, *I* can survive.

Q: Man was changed by his experience in the animal.

D: Of course he was changed.

Q: Does man, in a way, need to relearn and understand these feelings that became a part of him?

D: Yes, but will he? That is the question.

Q: Why didn't the spirit take over the birds, as it did the other animals?

D: Because the birds were so small. Some of the larger birds are quite intelligent, but they flew quickly and being in them was not as interesting as being on earth. Some spirits did enter birds, but they did not have as many problems as the ones who were in the animals. With the soaring and the gliding, it was easy for them to remember to glide out of the body and come back in, and glide away in astral traveling. There was not the entrapment, the fear, for they just melted away, and it was easier to get out.

❧

There are a few animals who will kill something and not eat it. They kill it to keep it out of their territory. There is a reason for that. They are the grumpy old men of the woods. It is better for the balance of nature that they kill something and leave it for animals who are not swift enough to kill, some of the weaker ones or the ones who truly need it at that time. It is not a waste, as when men shoot and kill something and leave it. Though it seems as if there is no need, there is always a need. A polar bear will not allow anything in its territory, even another female polar bear, until mating season. This is good, otherwise you would have many vicious polar bears on the earth. It is a way of nature controlling just how many there should be, so that they do not starve. Nature takes care of its own birth control with the seasons. You see what happens to the lemmings when it is a good year and there are too many; they rush to the sea for mass suicide.

Q: How did mental retardation begin, if spirits were perfectly balanced in the new bodies?

D: Mental retardation is not from the first world, it is from this world. In the beginning, there was no mental retardation. When an animal gave birth, if there was anything wrong with her children at all, the mother promptly killed it, because she knew it could not survive on the earth, and it would die sooner or later. So the mother pushed it away and did not feed it until it died or a predator came along and ate it. In nature it is the survival of the fittest. You will find very little mental retardation in wild animals. It is happening now with dogs and cats and horses that are inbred, that man has fooled around with. What man does not fool with is not tainted that way. If a kit or cub is lost and alone, sometimes it is healthy, but often there is a good reason why the mother abandoned it. If it is abandoned because the mother is dead, it is entirely different. But if the mother pushes it away, it is because something is wrong. Man tries to save everything that lives, and I am not commenting whether it is good or bad, I am just saying this is how it is.

Q: If the body initially lasted hundreds of years, what has happened to reduce its life span?

D: Sometimes it lasted up to a thousand years. It is because bad habits became so ingrained that it took longer to get rid of them. It is where deep-seated greed, deep-seated hate, deep-seated contempt, the opposite of deep-seated fear, perhaps even evil began. Some people are still today working out the marks that the spirits went back with at that time, because it had a thousand earth years to become deeply in-grained in the spirit, and it was that much harder to work out the karma. They decided it was easier for a lifespan to be between one day and ninety years. Some live to one hundred twenty-five, but that is not everyone. Actually, I would say the average lifespan on earth is one to sixty. A good figure. Many live over that, many do not make ten. They have found that a shorter course does not leave you quite as in-grained in wrong habits, or habits that you do not like. The longer you have bad habits on earth, the harder they are to break. Think of smoking ciga-rettes. If you have smoked for many years, it is hard to stop. Overeating is hard to stop. If you've done this for thousands of earth years, think how much more difficult it would be for the spirit when it comes back to stop overeating or smoking in the next lifetime. It was too long for the spirit's memory banks to work out, so the time was shortened.

Q: How does the body heal itself?

D: In the first lifetime, the creators of the body knew exactly what the blueprint of the body was and how to arrange it; how to arrange their own atoms and molecules, and the clay to build the body. If something went wrong they could look through the circuits, so to speak, change them, correct them, and change the animals. It was very easy. The spirits now have their bodies created for them. You do not create them yourself, and you do not care to remember where every tiny little nerve is. There is so much more for you to do. Trying to heal today is an entirely different problem. Healing then was very simple. It was with the mind. Some healers today remember how to heal some people. But they don't know what they are remembering each time. This is why they cannot heal every person.

Do not ever get discouraged if you are not healed, because there could be a karmic reason why you are going through it. It could be lessons you must learn. It is not *ever* a lack of faith in God. Do not allow people to say you are not healing yourself because you are lacking faith in God. People who have faith in God may say, "I am not healing, therefore, even though I believe in God, I must not deeply believe." They should not have to question. There is always a reason for an illness, and there is always a reason for a healing. There is always a reason for a miracle, so do not allow anyone to say, as a lot of your healers today do, "If you believed, you would be healed." Jesus did not say that. He said, "Believe and you will be healed." But he did not mean only in the body. He's talking about the spirit. The faith healers of today at times make it seem as if it is your fault you are sick. It is, but it is written. It is because you wish to learn a lesson, and they feel upset that you are not being healed. It bothers them. It should not, for any time someone lays hands on another, a healing takes place, whether it is in the body, in their energies, in anything, a healing takes place. It helps. That's what the Jewish people say, "It couldn't hurt."

Q: If we don't see well, is there a reason?

D: Yes, always.

Q: If we find the reason we don't see well, then we can have the eyes healed?

D: In some cases, but if it is written that the eyes are not to be healed, then they will not be healed. If it is written that they will be, they will be, and no one knows what is written, so do not ever give up. But do not get disappointed if what you are doing does not work and say, "It is because my faith in God isn't strong enough." Keep trying.

Q: Keep looking for the cause, the reason?

D: Keep working on the healing of it. Some people are born blind, who will never see. We cannot say to them, "If you find the reason, you will see." That is nonsense. There are no guarantees on earth, for no guarantees have been written in. You accept what you have. Thank God for anything that you do have. It is a lesson you are learning. Be pleased. Thank God you have this lesson. Thank God you have a chance to work it out, that He is giving, She is giving you a chance to work it out, and be happy with what you've got. Work on healing it. If it does not heal, do not give up. Do not get discouraged. If it doesn't work, at least you've strengthened something else. If it does work, then it is supposed to be.

❧

Q: Did the first spirits on the first earth experience fear of open spaces that we now call agoraphobia?

D: No. They came down in groups, and the animals did not ever have that fear of open places. Animals do not go anywhere that they fear. They stay away from it and do not even worry about it. Man feels he has to conquer. That is one of the phobias. Phobias are one of the things that animals do not have, except for hydrophobia, rabies, and that is a physical disease. The other phobias are mental diseases, but they came with time. The spirits who came directly into human bodies had no fears. The animal spirits who entered into animal forms are the ones who taught the human spirits who went in with the human forms. They taught them the fear and the greed. Human spirits did not have it, until they taught them. The first group who came down in the human body did not fear entrapment, for they knew they could leave and astral travel. What they worried about, of course, was that the body did not have a soul to keep it alive, and they would come back and find it decayed. That is why you may sometimes wake up suddenly in the night and check your body to make sure it's still there, that it hasn't decayed while you've been astral traveling. It was not a fear right away. It was a fear later on, until the souls were invented, or until they decided that they would take over the care of the body. It's not a job they have to do. It is a job they wish to do. Free will always.

An airplane pilot checks the airplane before taking it up, and this is what you did when you came back in your body. You checked it to be sure it was still there, still functioning. The first few times that the soul was taking care of it, of course, the soul very importantly said, "This is my body. I am the one who is going to check it and make sure you're taking care of it." That is what started the division between the ego and the consciousness, the spirit and the soul. A little bit of friction which lasts to this day.

Q: How were the spirits making their bodies from the elements of the earth?

D: They did it by the power of mind, concentration. The way you will eventually be able to. By concentrating, enough vibrations can go around and hold onto a table so it lifts up and moves; by just the power of concentration, by the gathering, by the creating, by thinking.

Q: If there is simultaneous time, how do you explain the reincarnation cycle?

D: There is simultaneous time only on our side of the veil, not on the earth. To get back on the earth, you have to be reincarnated. You have to go into a time zone, so to speak, for when you go into a body, from the day you go into it until the day you leave it, it starts dying. Everyone says it starts living, but from day one it starts deteriorating. As a baby it is growing, but it is still aging and deteriorating.

Q: Since earth is often harmful to man, are the planets more conducive to man's well-being?

D: To the spirit's well-being, some, yes. There are not always humans on the other planets, though there are some just like earth with people on them. But on some planets you are not human, you are your own spirit in whatever the lifeform is on that planet. In some you are not invaders, as you almost are on earth. You get along more naturally.

Q: When referring to up and down, are you using the Judaic-Christian concept of heaven being up and hell being down?

D: Yes, only to make it understood. It is neither, for as I said, we are *in* God, we are all *in*. There is no outside.

Q: That is the most powerful concept to grasp?

D: Yes, so you know you cannot fall, you move sideways.

Q: But we are always within God?

D: Yes, it is just that it is easier to look up and see the glory of the heavens. The sun brings living rays that make the earth green, therefore God must be up there sending it. The bowels of the earth are hot. They call hell hot. Therefore, it must be in the middle of the earth. No one has discovered where hell is. In the Bible they go down, but down would be the other side of the earth. It is probably in another dimension that would be sideways, down, up, it makes no difference.

For you are truly not alone. There are more dimensions. There are more people existing in this planet than can be counted or seen. In this room, right now, if a camera could photograph these spirits, you would not be able to count how many were in here. It is because the vibrations are not slowed down. They are here. You can feel them as warm spots. They let you know, at times, that they are here. But they are really here, and they are standing in between this, in here and around behind. They vibrate at a different rate, and that is the other side of the veil.

Humans came into their earth bodies and tried to convince the spirits in the animals not to reincarnate in the animal body. This was done, of course, with great difficulty and not with alacrity. It was done by trying to commune with the spirits, first of trees for they were easier to get to. Some of the spirits, though they were trapped there, enjoyed being there and did not want to come out. Some did, but kept saying, "How can we? We cannot get out. We are caught. We are trapped." The spirit in the human form said, "But you can do anything you want." And they said, "How can we get out? We cannot do it, no matter what you tell us." That started despair and feeling sorry for themselves.

Then the people decided they would try to contact the spirits that were in the animals. It was difficult contacting them while the animal spirits were in control. They decided to contact the animal spirits through mental telepathy, and then try to contact the spirits going along with the animals and trapped in the animal bodies. Now, of course, some of the animals said, "Go away, leave us alone. If they want to get out, they shouldn't have been here in the first place." Animals have compassion, yes, but to their own kind. Compassion for babies, for some other animals, but not for something that is going along with them.

People decided to work on the trapped spirits when the animal died and the spirit returned to the other side of the veil. Notice I do not say heaven or hell, but the other side of the veil. The veil could be right here in front of us and you just step through. When the animal died, we tried to tell them they did not have to go back, that they could choose to come in human form. Some of them agreed, and this was very pleasing, for this way they could learn love again. How lofty our ideals were at that time.

Some came back in human form, but they could not forget the animal instincts written on their spirits. They could not forget that they had to fight their way, that they had to steal from other animals. They were jackals. Jackals kill their own kind too, but sometimes they have to steal. Jackals are very fierce animals. They realized that even though the teachers from our side of the veil tried to program them, it was still written on their spirit, on the Akashic records, that when they came, they would steal. They felt no guilt: "I will steal it, it will be mine. I will get more than anyone else. I will sit on it, it may rot, but it is mine. I will not share it." They also had anger.

The "sons of God" were the ones who came down to teach them love. They did not know anger or greed. They came and created the bodies, first the human body. The ones who incarnated from the animal body into human body, but had the animal spirit in them, were the "sons of man."

The sons of man learned rape because of the animal during mating season. Males would have to attack other male animals for the female, and then cower the female into a corner and have his way with her. It was a form of rape; the female would be pulling away. When he came into the human body, this was the way he figured he had to mate, the same way. The animal instinct was in it, but corrupted because it was in the soul of man, who did not have to do this.

Murder came from being in the animal's body: kill or be killed. They went out hunting people, and of course they hunted and killed the gentle ones, the sons of God who would not hurt anyone. It is like Cain and Abel. One was the gentle one with the vines, the son of God. The other was the hunter, the animal, the son of man.

I am correlating the Bible with this to show you how it follows, but not to tell the whole story. There were still others left in the animal bodies, and the sons of God did a lot of mental telepathy while they were on earth, programming them: "You are not happy. You do not have to be caught." They started prayer and healing by sending out their energies toward them, and praying for them to stop despairing. But the ones who were in the animal bodies, watching what was going on between the sons of man and the sons of God, were not sure they wanted either one. For the sons of man were taking advantage of the sons of God who were gentle and loving.

This started karma, or lessons that needed to be

learned. What you give out, so you receive. The sons of man had to learn what they did to the sons of God. The animals with the human spirits in them were watching this, seeing the killing, and despairing more. They did not want what they were in, but they did not want to come back as sons of man. They did not want to come back as sons of God either, because they were the ones suffering and accepting it. This is the beginning of the Jews being the chosen, for they accepted, as the sons of God did, because they loved and they knew they could make their own body again. It hurt, but they could astral travel out of the hurt.

The human spirits in the animals watched this and knew that it hurt to die, and knew it hurt to be attacked, for they had picked up the feelings of the animal they were attached to. The only thing they could not do was tell the animal what to do, so some of them stayed in there for thousands and thousands of years.

The sons of man went about building things, and boasting of the kill or boasting of being king of the jungle, making a lot of noise. They came back with huge, giant bodies because they wanted to be bigger than anyone else. Of course, their ego was starting to be built up like the animal ego. They did not remember that the animal did that only when it was hunting and then lay down and forgot about it. What was written on the spirit of man was never forgotten. It could not be wiped out.

We, on the other side of the veil, looked and said, "We've messed this up a bit. God gave us free will and now we're misusing it. Everything out there looks so little, complicated, and messy. There is no plan. There is killing, raping, gluttony, stealing, and

picking on the sons of God. They are not understanding love." When the souls came back to our side
of the veil, we said to them, "It is chaos down there.
There is no plan, you are killing the animals, you are
discovering things, you are misusing your powers."
The sons of God must start using their true powers
of mental telepathy, telekinesis (which is moving
things), and the power of their mind to reach and
control the angry mass of the children of man—to
get through with prayers.

The children of God said, "Yes, our egos are not
that big. We can do this." They crossed over to the
earth domain and became a protected society of
priests, using their powers to overcome the other
minds and keep the masses down. Of course, the
ones who were human, the children of man, had
forgotten about the powers, forgotten how to use
them. This seemed like a good thing at this time. We
thought the children of God would use their powers
on the children of man, and the children of man
would understand. The children of man did not understand. Some became fanatics in following and
obeying the children of God. This gave some of the
children of God a very large ego. They said, "See, I
use my powers and they are all under my control. I
am the master, I am almost as good as God."

We looked from the other side and saw this wasn't
working either. We have got to have a different set of
rules, because now we have some children of God
who are being very good, and they are being persecuted, they are being killed. The children of man
are stealing from them and enslaving them. The ones
who call themselves priests are using their powers to
enslave the children of man. No one should be a slave
to another human, for God gave free will to every-

one. In the meantime, the children of men are re-membering some of the great and glorious things on our side of the veil and are saying, "We can create that, we can build buildings. We can make things. We can make this heaven. We can become our own gods. Why do we need God, for when we are God, we can create."

The children of man created many instruments for changing the weather and for driving out the priests. Then the priests started using their powers over the children of man. The children of man decided the children of God were good, and the children of God decided the children of man were evil, and that became the struggle of good and evil. But in doing so, the good had evil in them, and the evil had some good in them. When they died and came back to our side of the veil, we looked and thought it was time to end this world and start over again.

We decided to try and contact the most intelligent children of man and children of God. If they are listening they will prepare for the volcanic eruptions, lava and the fires; they should build tunnels into the cooler parts of the earth, caves. They must dig them down or find the natural caves, so that when it is over, they can start again. We from our side tried to contact them, for we could not go down and inter-fere, much as we cannot interfere now. But there were prophets. And we tried meditation. Some of the good who were very good listened; and some of the good who were not so good listened; and some of the bad who were not so bad listened. They went into caves and prepared themselves. Some of the oth-ers stayed, and of course that was their choice to do so.

CHAPTER TWO

The Second World:
The First Messiahs

WHEN THE VOLCANOES started erupting, the heat was oppressive. The tidal waves came, people died, the earth changed. Some of the people who picked the wrong caves were drowned, some of them who picked the right ones were saved. But it was by no plan, the first time around, of who should stay and who should go, and what was left was again the dark ages. The ones who emerged out of the caves were those you now call the cave men.

Now you ask, "Where did the intelligence go?" If you were in a cave and the whole earth changed, and you came out with only the few possessions you had in there, you could not turn on electricity. You could not drive a car, there was no gas. Your weapons soon ran out. You do not have the technology to make bullets, or to make steel. What could you do, except perhaps hunt to keep alive? Try to remember what a wild onion looks like, for a stew. You try to find clear water that does not taste sulfurous from the volcanic eruptions. Try to go someplace where it is not burnt and wasted, try to leave the desert areas, try to look for cool areas. You do not know which is north or south, everything has changed around. You were civilized people and all was taken from you. The first thing you thought of was survival. You must live, start again. You forgot how to create your bodies in the survival. You thought only of eating, drinking, and finding a place to rest. Now all of the animals were not killed, but when you came across the tracks of an animal, you had nothing with you. Your guns rusted away. You even forgot how to track animals. You've got stones, and you remember how to put them in an arrow shape, if you had the time to do it.

You remember that some of the people were very good, but some were very bad. When you came to caves where there were other people, you skirted them because you did not know whether they were good or bad, whether they would try to kill you as they did before, or what they would do. Now you are frightened. You no longer have the power. You no longer *need* the power, for the power had gotten you in trouble.

Now the plan was that if you were on earth, you must find your own way. The darkness came over your mind, to protect you from the power so you may survive if you wish. It became important to survive. It became a matter of manliness and womanliness to survive. It became an important thing, for we were the ones who were chosen to stay.

We heard there was a purpose. We must save the ones who are in the animals. We must save our friends. We must, because we want to. We will show them, though our powers are taken away; we are not stupid, we can remember.

And then, of course, the evil ones thought: "We will survive and wipe out every good person on this earth. This will be our planet, our earth. We enjoyed being animals. They took us out of the animal bodies. We do not enjoy being human, we will act like the animals, we will be animals."

Some who survived were the good, some were fearful, some did not know whether they were good or not. Some of the groups were trapped and killed by the evil ones, or the bad ones (because it was not evil, it was just bad and good). The bad ones killed some of them, but others escaped and decided, "We'll stock our own little bunch of rocks over here and the next time they come, we know how to play their game." That was the beginning of the first war on earth. The Bible calls it the war between good and evil. We call it "survival." At times a friendly group would come through, but you would not know and you would attack anything. The fear set in. You must stay in your own little tribes. You forgot about the animals who had human spirits then. You must survive, you must build up civilizations. You had dreams of remembering the quick life, electricity.

It was built up much the way it is here now, not quite as civilized, but perhaps even then some cities were more civilized. It was not a good thing and it was destroyed. It was not destroyed by God and it was not destroyed by us. It was destroyed by men working on the earth plane who tried to create bigger things and bigger weapons to harness energy of this type and that type. It's true that they could destroy the appearance of the world on their own, or destroy everyone on it that they did not like. They did in fact destroy the appearance of their own world. But no one can completely destroy the world except for God, and only when God is ready, when it wears out.

This is the second world we are into now, and it had to start as a stone age. People started trying to talk to each other when they met, rather than killing each other. It was not just grunts and groans as they say now, they had a language. Of course a lot of the large words, the sophisticated words, were lost in the language, because there were no such things as electricity or airplanes. It got down to the basics of shelter, clothes, and weapons. The language became smaller and smaller as the larger words were not necessary; language expands or contracts according to the needs.

One or two of the people would make friendly overtures, and this was good. Some of the tribes got bigger as they allowed others in. But sometimes people made overtures and were killed. They were surrounded by others, they started guerilla warfare and suspicion. Suspicion wasn't here before, but now they thought, "Do I trust this one, or don't I?" Then lying came in. The one who wanted to kill everyone would say, "I am your friend," and lying started.

Into this era came one of the sons or children of God who had the power and had not misused it. He traveled and preached, and told the people to pray. He told them not to worry about survival, that God would help them, and to trust in God. He got answers like, "Trust in God? What has God done for us?" But they had forgotten, you see. And through the generations some of the stories were passed on to their children, but some were not, and some were forgotten. He went from place to place, preaching. What he left behind was not so much the feeling of God, but a stirring of memories of past lives where things were better. Memories of how to start fires, and of people coming to them in the form of babies who grew up and would remember how to create metal, and what wheels are for to make it easier. The first group, before they had children and grew and formed tribes, did not have time for this. As the groups grew larger, the others who incarnated as babies came back with memories of what they were to do.

On our side, we started planning ways to help those on earth. When there were groups of about twenty, a storyteller was sent from village to village to tell them stories. In telling the stories, he brought back the memories. They would say, "Oh yes, yes, I remember." He went to as many places as he could, even to the bad ones, for he feared nothing and he loved all.

This was the Christ Spirit, the very first time around. He came in a storm, in the form of a story-teller. When he got to a village where there was much suspicion and much distrust, where the evil ones and the bad ones were, he said to them, "Trust in God. You do not have to kill your neighbors." He started much anger in the village, and he was killed. He was stoned, for that is all they had to kill with. Yet he went there, knowing he would drop a seed, that not all of them born to these tribes were bad. He knew the seed would spread to some who were good, and it helped make the evil ones less evil, for it awakened memories in some of them and they tried to be less distrustful of other people. Some of them had to go to other tribes, for they were thrown out of their tribes for being good. But the people in their tribe learned some goodness, for they threw them out of the tribe instead of killing them. They were beginning to learn goodness.

These were the years of fire, cavemen, so to speak, or the basics. People learned how to tend their gardens once more and grow things, to believe in God, and to defend themselves against others. It became more utopian. There were not many wars. People were finding peace. They remembered to make things, to paint, which they had not time for before, to dance and be happy. They started remembering God. They started remembering how to make clothes and weave, and not to be frightened of everyone. There were still pockets of tribes who were warriors or evil, who liked to hunt and kill, who liked to steal, who did not like to grow their own food.

Still some of the animals had spirits in them. And the world grew again, and it got larger. The buildings got stronger. The lights were lit in houses at night. There were defenses around the walls, and the prophets came, and people started with their power again. The power of remembering, the power of preaching, the power of healing; they had the power and they were going to use it. But they were going to keep it just for a certain class of people, and not allow the masses to have it. They were going to keep it for themselves, because the masses would misuse it. They used the power, and they used it very well, and the people grew.

The people prospered, until one of the men with the power looked down and said, "This is working very well, but I was not always the son of God. I started out as a son of man. It would be good to enslave these people, frighten them, and get everything I want out of them." He was cunning. He talked to the other priests gently and they did not know, for they truly believed that all was good and they were not looking for bad in the priesthood. They allowed him to take over, and he did many good things. He started the scientists working on things he remembered about genetics, perhaps even cloning. He had them turning the sons of man back into the animals that they were. Now this was a good thing because they learned how to reverse the processes in doing this. So the people who were in the animals could now, if they wished, come out and be saved, or become the children of man, or the children of God. Some of them came from gentle animals, and some came from fierce animals.

Now the people in the animals were watching this, for animals always watch people. They watched these experiments and thought, if it can be reversed, then we can get out, there is a chance for us to be more human if we want to. They watched the civilization and they liked it. They decided they would like to do this, and some were helped by the gentle doctors.

But some of the doctors doing these experiments almost went crazy with the power: "This is great. I can get rid of whoever I want, make them animals. I can get rid of the priests and I can become God." And the struggle started again between good and evil.

We watched from our side and knew we had to work out something better. We decided it would be best if we wrote the plan before we went onto earth, to see if we could live with that. The people who were evil or bad came to our side of the veil and said, "We're still not learning balance. Do you see what happened to us down there? Give us a little bit of power and we went crazy. What should I go back as next?" Next you go back so that there is no possible way you can get power. You need to go back blind. You go back mentally retarded. You go back crippled. You'll be born crippled. Go back so that you cannot have the power and you have to learn what it is like, and you can learn the balance. And they said, "That's a fantastic idea. That is the way to do it."

That was the start of babies being born blind, deformed, mentally retarded, deaf. It was their own idea, when they came back to our side of the veil: "You have to teach us how to grow. When we are healthy and we get the power, we run away with it. We are not learning anything. We are not learning balance, for all we have learned is evil. We must learn good, so that we do not come back and hurt." Remember they were truly from God in the beginning, and when they got to our side of the veil, it took a long time for them to get over the idea of their power.

Sometimes, they would jump right back in (incarnate into the earth plane) and get more powerful. But then when they came to our side we'd say, "You know you're from God. When you are on our side, it is love. You cannot be more powerful than God here, for we all have the same power on this side of the veil. It is only on earth that you can be stronger or weaker. On our side, we're all equal." And they said, "Come back, we must learn. So allow us to come in deformed and allow us to do this." Then we said, "That is a good idea. That is a perfect way, but remember, when you are born that way, it will not be easy. It will be a difficult thing for you to be born blind, or not be able to speak or think, and to be frustrated." And they said, "No, we can do it." When you get to our side of the veil, you forget all the deprivation and misery of earth. You are light, you are free. You are strong again, you can do anything. So we allowed the misshapen to be born, the lame and the blind.

When the first blind child was born, they did not know how to cope with it. The priest said it was full of evil spirits, and they killed it. The mother was heartbroken. After a while, the mothers started fearing the birth of their babies. Up until then, babies were all perfect. Now the mothers feared, not because their babies might be born blind or hurt, but because if they were, someone would say they were evil and kill them and the babies. And every mother wants her baby, no matter what it looks like. So the mothers started hiding away when they were pregnant, not telling anyone. They went into hiding, as they did when they were animals, giving birth in secret, for they were frightened, and they started praying, warding off the evil eye.

So we asked for deformities, and came down deformed. Men who called themselves priests said that God has cursed the mothers and destroyed their babies, had made them blind, because never before had there been any cursing like this. Always the people have been born healthy. And then they started saying, "You have sinned and you are women, you are the ones who have the babies. Therefore you and not man have sinned." It is the original sin. The first sin, because the first baby was born blind, the next one was born deformed. The priests claimed it could not be the male's fault, for the males did not have the babies. Therefore the mother, the one who had the babies, must have been the one who sinned. If she had not sinned, the babies would have been perfect as it always was. That was the start of blaming women for the first sin against God.

So the women ran off and hid with their children, and they protected them, and loved them. Then they started asking people who could heal to come and help their children, for truly a mother forgets karma, God, anything, but her child is most important. The mother felt as if indeed she had sinned. For if she had not sinned, how could she possibly have had a child that was not perfect, when everyone else's child was perfect. The guilt on that has lasted even until this day, so now we have guilt in the picture. You see how everything sneaked in there. Terrible guilt that they could have such children.

Some children were even born with scales, because the memory on the soul was transferred from the animals. All of the mythological creatures, centaurs and dragons, appeared on earth. Oh, the consternation that went on, the mothers crying and the fathers condemning. The priests decided they needed to appease God by sacrificing the sick children to God. Not the well ones, but the sick children, which made some mothers run even farther away. Some of the braver fathers went off and started their own small communities where they were gentle to the sick and the infirm, and took them in where they could find them. Some of the mothers who didn't wish to save their children if they were born blind or infirm or crippled would leave them out on the hills, hoping they would either fend for themselves or some kind stranger would pick them up. They would walk away and leave them so that they would not be condemned or beaten or forced to leave the community, and their husbands would not condemn them as evil and cursed. They did it for their own safety, to save themselves out of fear. What else could they do? Where could they go? Could they both die? No.

Could they bring their children into this world to have them sacrificed? It is a hard thing to take, so either you ran off with your child, or you let it die in the woods. Some of those children were found and brought to the villages, off in the distance, where they were cared for and allowed to fulfill their karma, to grow.

The so-called priests who were watching this said, "It's not working. The more we sacrifice the lame children, the blind children, the animal-like children, the more we're having. What we have to do, perhaps, is give God the most beautiful children as a sacrifice, and he will take this curse from us." So they started sacrificing the beautiful people, the gentle people. They took people from their own community, but also went to other communities and gathered captives, so the people would not grumble too much about killing the beautiful people. They did not sacrifice the men, because the men did not have babies. They sacrificed women, for the taint, the original sin was on woman, for women had babies. Women were born then, for a while, in shame.

It took them hundreds of years to accept the fact that the crippled and the blind are with us no matter what we do. Men somehow decided that having sex with women, which resulted in deformed children, was not a good thing. The men decided women were unholy, and it would be best if they did not marry them if they wished to be holy. Dedicating themselves to goodness and to staying away from women, men thought: "We men are much better, for we have not sinned. We will stay away from women and become priests, and only the ones who have animal instincts will be married to women. We will purify ourselves by staying away from all sexual thought."

Well, that proved more difficult for the man than he thought it would. He had to masturbate to satisfy the sexual drive, which other people said was very bad. When he was caught doing this, others tried to make him feel guilty: "You know you're not supposed to do that. You have given up all thoughts of sex, and sex is dirty. You do it with women. The women have blind children. You see what it leads to. You are sinning." You see what that led to. They put a natural act like that into sin, evil. The first sins, of course, that they wrote down had to do with sex, which was not a very smart thing to do. But they did it, man did it. God never said anything about sex.

God was amused, watching what was going on and waiting for someone to say, "Help me," but we did not. We stumbled, again and again, but we were enjoying ourselves. When you were living on earth it was not quite so funny, but we, watching earth experiments from the other side of the veil, were growing and learning. We tried to figure out how to unravel this mess that we started.

Men went into monasteries, and tried to give up thoughts of women. When women walked by and the men's thoughts were on women, the men started chastising themselves because they felt they were evil, and they wished to commit sins with women. They left the women with only a few men to share. So the women started prostitution, so to speak, because they had natural urges also, and with few men to share, they had to do exactly that. If they did not share, the birth rate would have gone down to zero, and we would have had to start again by creating other bodies. That was one step we'd already done; we'd found a beautiful working model we could easily use.

So the sexual urge was increased a little bit, rather than just the need to procreate, as the animals did every six months. The sexual urge was there to create often, so that the population would not die out. Or as the Bible says, "Go ye and populate the world," or some such thing. The urge was increased, and the women were again looked down upon, by other women this time. For the women who had their men did not wish to share, and those who did share were labeled prostitutes. They got their men behind them and persecuted the prostitutes. Now the men were torn between satisfying their needs in the nighttime and having to condemn these women in the daytime, because their wives would not get off their back.

Some men wished to go off and try to do without women. Other men said, "We will take multiple wives and we will tell our wives to be quiet. We don't want to be accused of doing things that are dirty or sinful, when it is natural. We will start taking multiple wives. We will put them in our group. We will take concubines or harems, mistresses or what have you; we will give them equal status." For a while that worked beautifully.

But the men in the priesthood, so to speak, were having a very bad time of it. The guilt started arising, they started making overtures toward their male companions. And the females in the harems started having sexual experiences with other women, because one man cannot keep five women happy. It doesn't matter how hard he tries, he could not keep them as happy as they wished to be. The need was there. It was not dirty. It was a need. It had to be done.

But when it was found out by some overpious people who were born with a lack of the sex drive, they got very upset and said, "If I can do it, why can't you? You have to live up to my standards or you are wrong." That is a very wrong attitude. Everyone has to live up to their own standards. When someone in power, a father, a mother, a priest, or king, says "you must live up to my standards or you are wrong," you feel demoralized. You can not live up to anyone else's standards of how to live. It is an impossibility. Each of you must set your own standards for yourselves, and not allow anyone else to put their standards upon you.

We on the other side of the veil watching this said, "They're doing it wrong again. We must send down a Christ Spirit again, in a man, to teach the people to look inside themselves, to raise their emotions, to find joy. But this time the world is a little larger, so instead of one, we will send three, in different times and different places." We sent a man and not a woman because they would not have accepted it from a woman. Not because we were discriminating on our side of the veil, but because we knew that a woman on earth would not have a chance to be listened to, no matter how right she was.

So we sent men to each of the three continents there were then, to travel and preach: "Do not worry about sinning, there is no such thing as sinning. The Father, the God, He forgives all. He has created you. *If you feel that you need to ask for forgiveness, ask and He will give it to you*. That is very important. Not that you have to ask, but if you feel you need to ask, then ask and it will be forgiven you. It is important to enjoy life, not to hurt anyone, to treat each one as you want to be treated. Not as they treat you, but as you would want them to treat you. Love one another, even the sick, and the ones who sin, for God is love. Forgive yourselves, and grow and enjoy."

They came down and they preached, and some people listened and they wrote some of it down. When they approached the priests, the priests got frightened, for they were teaching fear and not love. The Christs were killed, not all at the same time, but they were killed. And as happens to writings and to word of mouth, the messages got changed through the years. Some began saying, "If you wish forgiveness, you must go through my God. If you wish forgiveness, you must do this, you must do that, and if you do not, God is an unforgiving God."

We looked down from our side and said, "What kind of planet is earth, that we get so involved in it we forget all our good ideas and good intentions. Even when we get there, we do not listen to our inner selves. This is a puzzle we must figure out."

We watched, and again they built a civilization. And again the civilizations were destroying each other. Again they were warring, and this time they were finding bigger and bigger things to fight with. (This is what you are doing right now. Fortunately, you are proceeding at a slower rate.) The people didn't care if they all died. Eventually life on earth was destroyed, but this time the desolation was caused by pollution. Everything was laid waste, nothing grew where the battles were. The people died of starvation, plants died, animals died. The desert started. The sun, from all the nuclear power that was sent out, shifted the earth a little bit on its axis. The earth moved closer to the sun, and everything slowly died, except for a few hardy people.

CHAPTER THREE

The Third World:
Playground of the Gods

T HE ONES who had the knowledge were directed on a trek. Some were good and some bad, for we knew that a balance was needed if the earth was to work out its problems. If it was all good, the people who were still on our side could not come back as bad, to work out their karma. It *had* to happen. Each one had to have a chance to bloom. On their trek they moved away from the desert areas toward a jungle. When they got there, there were very few of them remaining, but enough to start.

These were no longer cavemen, but tree dwellers. They built platforms in trees to be above the animals. They brought much knowledge with them. They brought their cooking implements, books, and clothing. But in a steamy jungle, the cooking pans rusted, the clothes rotted, the books decayed, and they had to start again from the knowledge they had in their minds. Where to find things in this different world that was open to them? I think they were near the equator. (The equator was not in the same place then as it is now, but that kind of jungle.) The animals grew quite well there. The people had again to

75

survive and start over. In the jungle atmosphere, though there were poisonous things, snakes and what have you, it was not a harsh reality. Food grew in trees, it was almost a paradise. They would not get as greedy, and yet, we could come in as bad and good, and start all over again, gently.

We are in the third world now. When civilization started growing, we sent down men and women who were half God and half human to direct the people. That way, being half God and half human, they would not forget what God was, and what they were there for. Then the people would listen, would they not? So we sent down those the Greeks called the Gods of Mount Olympus to help them. We sent them down to three different places again, around perhaps where China would be, where the Greeks would be, and around where America would be. We were taking parts of the power of God and putting it into a human being, who was then more than human. We put them on the mountains and hoped this would work this time.

The people came to them and asked them what they should do, and the Gods helped them for a few centuries. Then the Gods on earth started squabbling among themselves over who was the better God. On our side of the veil, we realized this was not going to work. We have not yet figured out what to do. The Gods are helping, but now they are quarreling among themselves. They are picking up the earth feelings, and they are becoming more manlike than Godlike. They are making themselves too important. They are forgetting their missions. We must again let the earth come to its ultimate conclusion and destroy itself, and start over. Now when I say destroy itself, I mean destroying most of the people that are there, in their own way, and humans manage to do this very well.

We watched the Gods play their games with the humans, and we decided never again to give so much power to any human that it is half God and half human, for the earth corrupts even them. The human beings managed to destroy themselves again, this time with sickness. The sickness came from our side of the veil. It came from our people, who said, "The people down there are either born healthy or unhealthy, but they are not sick. The world polluted itself, there are germs that can infect the human body. We must now take away the shield that protects the human body, so that man can be brought to understand pity, understanding, sympathy, and love, for there is a lack of it." The well ones had no sympathy for the sick. (Even today you will find that those who are always healthy have a great contempt for people who get sick. It is from that time.) We decided the people needed understanding, so Pandora opened her box, and out came sickness. That way man could learn compassion for the weaknesses of others. By this time, the ones on our side of the veil were wrapped up in the idea of going back to earth and learning by punishing themselves. They felt the only way they could possibly learn anything was to be sick, to be upset, to be blind. Perhaps you would say we were wrong. But you are back in your human bodies to do the same thing. We enjoyed it. As a matter of fact, some of us cannot wait to be born again, to try, for it is fun.

Sickness came into the world, and people did not have compassion for other people. The doctors did not try to find answers. They were still interested in getting the human spirits out of the animal bodies, not curing sicknesses. Sickness was something new. Again a taint, again a curse from God. Poor God, who has not been asked yet, who is sitting there watching. God has been blamed for many things that God did not do. The only thing that we could possibly blame God for is giving us our free will, so that we could make a mess out of things and try to straighten them out, as best we could. But in all of this, though to you it may seem a hodgepodge of give and take, this and that, a pattern is emerging from our experiments. Our creativity is growing, just from being on earth and from being on our side of the veil; from watching, we are ever growing and ever learning. If you remember, in the beginning, before we came to earth, we knew nothing. We just watched, and were curious. Now our spirits have grown so we know the difference between positive and negative, between love and hate. We have had many lessons imprinted on our souls, on our spirits. We have lived. We have tasted the fruits of everything that is on earth and found them good.

CHAPTER FOUR

The Fourth World:
Lemuria, Atlantis, and Egypt

N OW WE WILL GO into the fourth world. The Greek Gods were not totally destroyed, but they became more human than Godlike in the fourth world. We brought the unicorn with us for its beauty and its whimsy. We brought into the fourth world all the best and the worst of the other worlds. We mixed them up to see if we could find a medium, to have human beings with human frailties, but also human goodness. So the good are not so good, and the bad not so bad, but people on their way to being well-balanced.

We decided that when we go down to earth, we should bring two friends with us in case we forget why we went down. A trinity, so to speak, in the spirit world that we would be sure to listen to, for they are our friends. They know the plans, and they are to help us. They are guardian angels, guides, teachers, friends, whatever you wish to call them. They are the ones we listen to in lifetimes. We were sure we could have a direct line to them, and that they would help. We decided to write our life plan, knowing if we stuck to it, things would work out.

The fourth world was a tangled world. Though we looked to God in ourselves for the answers, the answers were not so easy anymore. It would have been easy in the beginning, but we got so involved. There were so many threads leading so many directions, that to straighten it out completely, some of us would have to go against our will. It would have to be ended completely, with no one on earth. All the spirits who were on earth would have to work it out on our side of the veil, and not be afforded the school that earth was.

Lessons would take longer to learn, but it could have been straightened out by wiping out man completely, and not even starting again. But a lot of people said, "Now wait a minute. It is my life. It is my free will. If I wish to go down there and work out my problems, I have the right to do so. If we ask God's permission and this is the only way that it can be over, then we will lose our free will. Our guides remind us that God is here at all times." So we came down into the fourth world again, with our guides to listen to, and we found that when we again got into the mystique called earth our guides could not contact us so easily, for we paid very little attention to them.

It was written on our souls what was to be done, what we did. We brought that back with us. What happened to our bodies was of no concern to us ever. We cared for our bodies, yes. We respected our bodies, for they were our vessels to use. They were our clothing to use. And some started abusing the body, not taking as good care of it as they should. Some even had a contempt for the body. Before, there was never a contempt for our bodies. For others, yes, but not for our own, not because we were unhappy with the way our bodies looked. We were unhappy with the nagging of our spirits telling us what we should do, so we tuned them out. But our spirit guides would not give up. Our higher self, when we went to sleep or when we meditated, said, "Please help. You know how to get through to the conscious, if you can," They tried and tried and could not. There was a void between God, spirit, and man. The fourth world was an empty world when it came to God. People abused their own bodies. There was overdrinking, overeating, Sodom and Gomorrah, perhaps trying everything with no conscience to guide us.

We decided to slowly bring guilt into the world. It was not a good thing to bring in, but we felt we needed a red flag so the people would know when they did something wrong. Until that point, no one felt guilty. We slowly brought guilt into the world, and it worked very well for a while. People would say, "Ah, I've done something wrong and I will not do that again."

Still the void was there, between man and God. For we knew that if we asked God, He might end the world. Then we could not have the earth to learn lessons with. Some of us on the other side of the veil said, "This is nonsense. Of course we must invoke God. We must ask God's help, for we cannot do it on our own any longer. Now we truly need God. There must be a closer spirituality. From the first world to this, we have drifted so far from God that we have thought *we* were Gods, rather than collectively we were God."

So we sent in people with mediumistic powers, contacts between one world and the other, such as the instrument here. We sent prophets, people who could foretell the future, and since the plans were written it was easy to foretell the future. Slowly, people were being brought back to the thought of God.

Then the prophets became as bad as the priests. They also became corrupt. Not all, but most. False prophets came in saying, "We know what the future is. We can manipulate to get what we wish on earth. Who cares what happens when you die. We are alive. We want to amass fortunes. We want our own way. We will build our lives so that we are even more important." By invoking the name of God, the priests, prophets, and mediums became all-powerful. They could see into the future, so the people came to them daily, weekly, monthly, and they had complete control over their lives. Sometimes they lied and told people, "If you give us our proper reward, enough money, we can change the future," which was entirely nonsense. For they told them the wrong future, and after getting a reward they changed it to the true future, and they had the people under their thumb. The prophets and priests became people with great karmas to work out.

We looked down and some said, "Perhaps we have failed again." But others diagreed: "No, we have not failed. We are getting a pattern down. With each different world, though, we seem to be going farther away from God, farther away from ourselves, farther into cruelty, war and destruction. This is what earth is, a learning. The teachers are learning, and the pupils are learning. Let us continue, do not totally destroy. Let us continue."

This is where the fear came in that someday God will end the world. From this time on, prophets were always saying that in the year so and so, the world will end. They are taking it upon themselves to be God. No one knows if God will end the world, or when. He has not taken any of us into His confidence, or Her confidence, into God's confidence. Only God knows, for He created the worlds, and if the time comes that it will wear out, that is in God's timing, not our timing. No one can predict or foretell.

The predictions are not coming from God. They are coming from us, who are on the other side of the veil. They are coming to mediums and prophets, who are perhaps misreading. An end of the world as you know it now, perhaps. But the world ends often, as you know now. It ended in the nineteen hundreds. It ended in the eighteen hundreds. Entirely different worlds emerged from what was in the beginning, but the end of earth as a whole, only God knows. He is not a cruel God. The people who invoke God's name in this and that make Him a cruel God, but He is not. People are cruel to each other, but God did not make them so. They made themselves so.

Now we go to Atlantis, Lemuria, and the beginning of this time. You may ask where this section of the first world was, that section of the second world, this section of the third world. A lot of them are now under the ocean. A lot of them are where the poles are. The earth is always changing on its axis. It is always going a little bit off, it always has, it always will. It is in a slightly wobbly motion. The changes, the earthquakes, the volcanic eruptions, the ever changing core of the earth has pushed land up and pulled it down. The earth is not a stable planet. None of the planets are stable, except perhaps the moon, which is what they call a dead planet.

The starting of Atlantis and Lemuria was the beginning of the fourth world. There were also people where Egypt is now, and a few other places, but we start with Atlantis and Lemuria because they became sophisticated. Even back then, those with a scientific mind knew that Atlantis and Lemuria could become quite famous. The people in Egypt and other places were a more gentle people, not quite scientific. They were content to let the land alone and live with it, and love it. Atlantis and Lemuria were slowly building up from the jungle men, becoming sophisticated. They started pottery, meditation, and making things.

Again the evil started with people, with the mediums, with the prophets, the foretellers of doom. Atlantis started corrupting itself from the inside, and the prophets got extremely greedy: "We will run the world. I will be the greatest priest or medium. Everyone will bow down to me. I am God." This is when God put his foot down, so to speak, and said, "I am the Lord, thy God. Thou shalt not have strange gods before Me." And we realized that we were making ourselves Gods, or allowing others to make themselves God, when truly, they were nothing but God's creation, or *in* God. It brought us up short.

That commandment does not mean the Buddha was not God quality. The commandment means there is only *one* God. You shall not make a man a God. You shall not make even Jesus the Christ a God. They were *sons* of God, to bring God to you. They are not God. They are like you and I. Merely sons and daughters of God. They were bringing the Christ Spirit, or the spirit of God down. But you in this world have again made of Jesus a god, Moses a god, Buddha a god, Confucius a god, Hitler a god. Sometimes of your husbands and wives a god, prophets a god, mediums a god. They are merely a contact with God. They are not anything more than mortal human beings, bringing the word of peace and love to you.

We sat by and allowed Lemuria to destroy itself, hoping Atlantis would say, "See, we are learning." But the scientists rushed into Atlantis, because it was a great time for them. They had artificial limbs and eyes. They could change people back and forth. They could make them animals, they could make them vegetables. They could make them anything they wanted. They could make a banana just by thinking about it. They could make wheat just by thinking about it. It was an exciting time. The power of the mind was back. There were many arguments between mind powers, between minds, between people who thought they were gods.

The good people, who listened to the pure prophets, tried to save Atlantis and could not. The others pooh-poohed and said the pure prophets were wrong. But the gentle people listened to the pure prophets, and they started leaving with their airplanes. They started flying to where the Mayans were, and to where the Egyptians are now. Some flew to where the Eskimos are today. They flew all over.

The people from Atlantis, the ones who were trying to save the rest of the world, knew they had to colonize outside of Atlantis to save themselves, and perhaps start something good. They left the mad scientists behind, hoping that when they destroyed themselves, the shock of seeing everything blow up in their faces would go into their spirits and cause them to be careful the next time they came around. Some flew to other planets (there were interplanetary

friendships at that time) and some to other lands.
They set up runways and brought the good with
them. They brought the good mediums, the good
prophets, the good priests, and they watched Atlantis
destroy itself.

The minute Atlantis was destroyed, the planes
could no longer fly, for that was their base of opera-
tions, that was where they were getting their energies from. But they brought machines with them,
fantastic machines that could be run for hundreds
and hundreds of years without being recharged.
They brought healing machines with them. They
brought with them only the good out of Atlantis, for
this time, the evil that was in Atlantis and Lemuria
went down with it.

This time, we did not allow the bad to survive
with the good. Only the good survived from Atlantis
and Lemuria, but remember they were migrating to
lands where there were still people. They were not
migrating to lands where there were souls that were
unevolved. Some of them were highly evolved, gentle souls. Some of them were warlike, but none perhaps as vicious and God-forsaken as Atlantis was.
For truly, Atlantis and Lemuria were written in the
Bible as Sodom and Gomorrah.

All men are warlike, as you can tell, even living in
your own family. When you can stop becoming angry at your loved ones in your own household, and
that includes your children, your in-laws, your husbands, your wives; when you can live a lifetime
without once being angry at anything, then you are
succeeding in finding peace on earth and spreading
it out. Everyone wishes for peace on earth, but they
are not starting with themselves. They wish others
to find peace, but they get angry with their best

friends, with their loved ones, with other people. Anger that is inside you goes out and multiplies, and this is why earth is a warring planet. It is from each of you, and I mean everyone on this earth. Even the ones who say they are truly at peace. When they get angry at *anything*, including themselves, war starts again. And you can see it will take a long hard time for peace to come to this earth, for everyone must realize it starts with themselves. People who wish to go to other lands to help bring peace must first bring peace to themselves, to their loved ones, to the people around them before they can go off to bring peace to other people. Not until we have children who are born into peace and do not ever know anger, can there truly be what you call peace on earth. God never promised peace on earth. Jesus perhaps promised peace to men of good will, but *not* peace on earth, to everyone.

The Bible is a rough outline of creation started by Moses who began the Jewish religion, and I was the first and perhaps the last king of the Jews. The Jewish nationality and the Jewish religion started with Moses. It was not before. It came after he had a vision, and he saw, and he started writing the tablets. The Bible is a good book, but it is not the only book. I'm not putting down anyone's religion. I am saying that it is an addition to other religions. It is just a book. The true religion is written in your hearts, if you allow it to come to the fore. Many people are afraid to allow it to come to the fore, because they are afraid of what others have done, and what they will do.

I say this to you: Do not ever be afraid on earth, for the earth is only a school. You have been here many times. You have been here so long, you have lost the joy of it. *Do not lose the joy of living.* Do not allow yourselves to become another Atlantis, for they forgot the joy of living and became tied to material things. They lost contact with the idea that you are here for only a few years. In Atlantis, they believed that their knowledge would allow them to live and live. But that is taking over God's job, and God would not allow that. For when you live on and on, you tend to feel you are God. And as the commandment says, "*I* am the Lord, thy God." You are just God's friends.

When the Atlanteans went into Egypt, the prophets and the priests and the ones who were close to God, they decided to set up a monument to God. They built the pyramids using their ingenuity, their mind power, their beauty, and their astrological readings of the stars. By using their powers, they were able to make something that weighs ten thousand pounds weigh nothing. They built the pyramids to outlast man, and we feel that they may, for the pyramids have maybe eight to twelve thousand million years to go yet. I mean the ones that were created by the ex-Atlanteans and Lemurians, not the ones that were created by the men. There are a few who tried to imitate and couldn't do so. The pyramids were not made for the kings to be buried in. The pyramids were raised so that people could see them and thank God, or raised as a prayer of thanks to God. They didn't care what people thought about them. It was for God they were made, not for man. As earth was made, *not* for man.

When the Atlanteans went into Egypt, the Egyptians were not yet highly evolved, spiritually, mechanically, or scientifically. The Atlanteans looked at them and said, this is the promised land. We will help them, but we will not make them slaves. We will not take over. We will not be gods. We will help them. And they started healings with the ankh, a symbol of life that came from Atlantis with other tools.

As time went on, the Egyptians raised the Atlanteans from just ordinary human beings or missionaries to priests and God and Pharaohs and kings. We looked down and saw it starting all over again. But the Atlanteans proved they had had enough of being gods. When they ruled, they were gentle rulers. They were holy people. They were in contact with God; it was a spiritual world. They themselves did not fail this time.

They started to fail when they began intermarrying with the Egyptians, and this is where interracial marriages started getting a bad name. The Egyptian wives and husbands, who had not lived through the chaos of Atlantis, started having ambitions. And though the Atlantean mothers and fathers tried to teach their children peace and love, the Egyptian mothers and fathers started teaching greed: "You can be king, look at what you can have. Look at what your father is throwing away. They wish to give him gold and he does not want it." The children were pulled in two directions, and the Atlanteans said, "You see, intermarriage is bad." And so it was written in books that intermarriage is wrong. Of course, in all the other worlds they intermarried and it was nothing. This is where intermarriage between the races first started. You still find it today. You find it in every land, because of that. It was when children started being born deformed again.

The Atlanteans and Egyptians were truly all of the same race. The Atlanteans were lighter. Most of them had light skin, blond or dark hair, and blue eyes. The Egyptians were darker, from light to black. Now, no one said anything about light and black Egyptians intermarrying, for they were all Egyptians. It was just marriage between Atlanteans and Egyptians, no matter what shade of color they were, that was wrong.

ಿ

Q: I understand that Bermuda and Atlantis were somehow together at one time.

D: Bermuda was one of the higher mountains that did not go down, yes.

Q: So what we call the Bermuda triangle today was part of Atlantis?

D: Yes, and some of the time machines had not been turned off when it went down. They had time machines, forward and back. In the Bermuda triangle, at times, that time machine sends things forward or backward into time, to disappear forever from this time.

Q: Are the spirits completely out of the animal and tree bodies?

D: No, but we must save that for Atlantis and the early migration to Egypt where the body perfectionists were. They worked with the scientists to change and alter the bodies, until finally they were freed, with the determination never to return again and be entrapped in the animal bodies. They go along with them and enjoy them, but they will not be entrapped again, for they are too smart now to do so.

Q: You referred to the five endings of the world. Is this then a sixth world?

D: No, this is the fifth.

Q: Then we are actually in Noah's world, as Noah and the ark was the fifth. So we are in the fifth world.

D: It is Noah and the ark, and also Atlantis. All at the same time.

Q: So there were four endings, and we are in the fifth world?

D: Yes.

Q: I had a question. We talked about the Greek Gods in the last session. Can I assume that the other groups living on earth at the same time developed their own Gods?

D: We call them the Greek Gods in mythology because that is the only group of Gods that have come down this far. In the Hawaiian islands, they had Pele, the Fire Goddess. They had their own Gods and their own names. They had Oden, and the Gods of China came through. All of the Gods truly were.

Q: Was mythology a reality at one time?

D: Yes. Everything that has been read, that is imagined, either comes from this planet or other planets. The animals and humans combined, space travel, science fiction—have all happened or will happen perhaps in other worlds. Imagination is not so much imagining, but picking up stories that are there, and have happened.

Q: Are UFOs only in our imagination?

D: No, they are real. Some are space probes. Most have robots in them at this time, until they can analyze the atmosphere.

Why is it so unbelievable that they would be coming to visit us when we are sending probes to Venus and Mars? It is the same thing. Are they more intelligent than us, on their planet? No, they are as intelligent as we are. Are they more advanced than us? Some are older civilizations, but not more advanced, or not more technological, because we have sent up space probes in other worlds that we have had. Some of them are even some of ours returning.

Q: When we talked about planets, were you referring to the solar system of which we are a part?

D: No, to all of the solar systems. We spirits move faster than the speed of light. We just think and we are there. That is faster than the speed of light, and soon again, man will be going faster than the speed of light. That is no problem. It is very simple. They will wonder why, after they have done it, why they did not figure it out before. But it is not the time.

This time, we from this side are trying to slowly spoonfeed knowledge to earth, slower than we did in the other worlds. Perhaps we will slow the ending of the world again, and instead advance it to where it should go. We are trying to deter man from trying to destroy himself. God is not destroying man. Man is trying to destroy himself again. Most human beings now are born with a death wish. It is the wish to get back to our side of the veil and be where you belong. It is homesickness, but when you are on our side, you wish to get back on earth and do it. We are complicated spirits, because we have great intelligence and our intelligence keeps us ever curious. When you get on earth, you lose some of your curiosity. That is why boys try reckless things like climbing trees and lighting fires, ever curious and ever wishing to return, a suicide wish.

Q: I wonder if you could talk a little more about thought and creation?

D: Of course. As everyone knows, it is no secret. One has said, "Mind is the builder," but actually, "Mind is the creator. As you think, so shall you create." Not so much shall you do, but shall you create, for you, with your thoughts create your future, create things to be, and things that were. You are creators, for you create your lives. You create joy, happiness, sadness, misery. You create your own illnesses. You create your own problems. *No problem has ever been created for any human being on earth.*

Every sickness, every problem is created by yourself. It is a difficult pill to swallow. It is easy for you to say, I raised a son or a daughter, and they did this to me, and now they are creating problems for me. It is nonsensical, for you created that child and drew it to you, and raised it. You therefore created the problem from the beginning, and all problems that come from it, you created. Why did you create it? For lessons you wished to learn. But every problem you face, even tripping over your own shoes in the morning, is a problem you've created for yourself. You are the one who put the shoes there to be tripped over, or married the person who left the shoes there to be tripped over. When you start realizing that you create your own problems, then you can start creating situations to help and aid you. Man creates by thinking, for truly mind is the creator. Mind is the spirit. You think about something and then go about creating it. Much as you create a dress from a piece of material, putting it together and creating it, so do your thoughts, for actually you are using power of mind to make your body move, to help you create. But everything you do is creativity, from cleaning house, to making food, to working, to praying, to healing, to making yourself sick. It is all created by you. So rather than mind being the builder, mind is the creator. For that is all you are, a creator. You have created your life on earth. You have created problems. You have created joy. You have created everything. For you are from the Creator, God, who thought of you, and so you were; and as you think, so you do. You cannot say you are a destroyer. Some people think the opposite of creating is destroying. Nothing is ever destroyed. It is ever created, ever upward. You may create havoc, you may create destruction, you may create hell, but you are creating always. Never destroying, for nothing can ever truly be destroyed. Changed, but not destroyed. It is always there. Nothing ever goes into nothingness. There is no such thing as nothingness. Once something is created, it may be changed, but it is always there.

Q: Was all this thought created before we wrote up our story, before we came into earth to have our experience?

D: Yes, of course. It was created in the beginning.

Q: It's not being created at this moment then?

D: Yes. [Laughter.]

Q: What is the difference between the two?

D: In the beginning, there was God. God created by thought, souls and spirits all at the same time. And from there, constant thought changes and creates always. It is never void. It is constant change, constant creation.

Q: The ability to think, then, was created in the beginning.

D: Yes, for you are just thoughts of God. If God stopped thinking about you, perhaps you would no longer exist, for you and earth and everything are just a thought. You are because you were thought of. Just like this house. If it was never thought of, it would never be. Is that not so? You were thought of, and you are. You are a part of God, you are within God. Nothing is without God. Nothing is outside of God. Everything is within. Every thing that you consider insignificant is significant, because it is a part of God. It is within God also. It is a whole, within a whole.

CHAPTER FIVE

The Fifth World: Recorded History

W E TALKED about the end of the worlds and the beginning of this world. It's not the final world, but it is the world you are living in. The last time the world ended, or most of the world ended, most of the people were returned to our side of the veil, to where they were created, where they belonged, back here to start over again. Not everyone was taken. Each time the worlds have come to an end, so to speak, there have been civilizations left over. There have been people left over. There has been knowledge left over, and it is important that the knowledge went from person to person. If it was not written down, it was handed down by word of mouth.

I want to start with the pre-Atlanteans, from the end of the last world to the beginning of this, when it was not quite built up. The building up took many thousands of years. In each of these, they brought along their knowledge: the knowledge of healing, of mathematics, of astrology, all the important things. Some were back to cavemen types, some were back to small native tribes. But others still carried the intelligence with them. Noah and his family, and two of each kind of animals, brought all the knowledge with them. This goes along with the Bible that you are interested in. This also goes along with the creation stories of the Orientals and the Indians. Throughout the world, they all told the same story. It's all the same story from the beginning.

It is hard to explain why civilization remained in some places, while in others a lot was wiped out. We have tried to explain this with the ending of the world. At times the whole world was almost completely wiped out. A few times, a civilization flourished while others were just about wiped out. They lost complete contact. But they brought with them, as always, the knowledge. They brought with them the important astrological knowledge, mathematical knowledge, and the building knowledge. We did not start out on earth knowing nothing. We started out knowing everything. We brought all of these things with us. At times our minds were so powerful we could end forty people's lives if we wanted, just by thinking of them. Our minds were that powerful.

The stories were not written for us the way we should have written them. God allowed us to go our own way. We decided, en masse on our side, to write the story in advance so we had at least some knowledge beforehand where we should fit in, something to act out. We decided what we would like to work out for balance. Everyone says they are striving for Godliness. God is perfect balance, yes? So we are striving for balance, to be Godlike, to be perfectly balanced. We looked back on the Akashic records, on our own stories, to find things we were unbalanced in, or things we should not have learned or done. We put events into the story to balance it out. Sometimes the lives we led were very humdrum: slaves attached to galleys, or peasants in front of a plow, just pulling endlessly back and forth, day by day, to make a living. Very tedious, but we learned so much.

We decided, after the last time the world came to an end, that this is what we would strive for. We would also strive to bring the knowledge to everyone on earth. We all started with it on our side of the veil. We wanted to bring it to earth for the good of mankind. Each time we thought this time we are going to make it.

Well, I'm sure you know we haven't made it yet. Again, we humans of earth, when we get into the human shell, get an amnesia. Besides, we have a different direction to go. Up until Atlantean times, it is a mundane picture of enlightenment, of growing, of building: building cities, building airplanes, building telephones, electricity. Yes, all of the things that you have now, some even better. We had lights that did not cost as much as you pay now. The electricity at that time was from a much better source, a much cheaper source. And we knew all of the healings. We still do.

This lasted until the corruption of the white people, who were powerful and more angry than the Atlanteans. Atlanteans were gentle loving people, who were easily influenced by a more powerful race. The Atlantean civilization was growing, as well as that in Lemuria, Mu, and five or ten others. Egypt, India, and China were also cradles of civilization. Then there were the cold countries, where the Norsemen and the Englishmen were, where the Tartars were, the harsher countries. From the harsher countries you get harsher people. People who have the will to survive, even if they have to kill other people and put them under their yoke. They do not trust people who are gentle, who are kind, who are following God's word, who feel: "I know I am good. If you kill me, you are only killing my body. You are not killing my spirit, you are not killing my soul. You cannot hurt me that way. I will say yes sir, no sir to you. I will not fight with you." The Atlanteans would not fight. People came on a boat from one of the colder countries, and saw all of the marvels that were there. They brought Atlanteans back to their country to build up these marvels.

After two or three thousand years their countries were built up, with the Atlanteans running them. The people in the colder countries began saying, "Why, the Atlanteans are running our religion, they are telling us how to believe. We are as intelligent as they are. They are showing us the stars, and teaching us, but we are smarter than they are. We are more powerful, we can kill them and they do not care. We will take over what they have done. We do not need them. We have learned all there is to learn."

They killed all Atlanteans except for the ones that intermarried, the children of man intermarrying with the children of God. Atlanteans were the children of God, the colder people were the children of man. The intermarried ones were spared, but the pure ones, the priests, the ones who had the intelligence, were killed. Then the people found that they did not have the power, they did not truly learn everything, as most people who are impatient. They did not know the full details behind everything. They knew the surface, but when you just know the surface, you do not know how deep it is. So everything went to ruin.

The same thing happened in the Mayan countries. The Indians there thought they could take over and be as good as the Atlanteans. They intermarried in South America, all along the Polynesian islands, Easter Island, all of those places. The Atlanteans went to many places all around the world.

Some of the places, like Egypt, India, and China, accepted them gently. They said, "Yes, the Atlanteans are going right along with the teachings, with what our masters had brought down, with what we have saved, with ancient files of the ancient writings, with the stories." They accepted them gratefully and were nice to them.

But then there were those who did not accept the Atlanteans: the South American Indians, the whites in the colder places, and the Indians in this country. They got rid of the Atlanteans. When you feel some-one else is smarter than you, and perhaps you feel they are laughing at you, treating you like a child, you want to strike out, so you kill them. The Atlanteans and the Lemurians, the Mu's, all of them did not fight back, they were not an aggressive people. They were destroyed eventually. They intermarried in some places, but the intelligent ones were de-stroyed because of their goodness, because of their knowledge. Somewhere a witch doctor or other doc-tor said, "You are a threat to me. Everyone pays attention to you, you have all this and I have nothing. But I am as smart as you. I will kill you and then they will look up to me." When he kills that one, he loses the knowledge that is so important.

Atlantis created an interchange of knowledge be-tween the people from South America and the cold countries of Europe. They brought people from one country to the other, doctors from India to teach them. When others got to Atlantis, they were upset over the Atlantean superiority, and that the

Atlanteans would not go beyond their powers. The Atlanteans would not play God, because they knew the earth would be destroyed if they did.

But the ones that came over, the young scientists who were just starting to learn, they were the ones who said we must go further. We must look further, we must investigate further. We must divide the atom. We must divide the crystal. We must see how far it goes. The Atlanteans said, "We know how far. You have gone far enough." And they said, "Oh, you are old men. You have an old civilization, you are stagnant. We need young blood, a young country, where the older people are pushed aside for the younger people." Only the young feel they know it all, and only the young can destroy, because they are not intelligent enough in age and maturity not to do something rash.

In Atlantis, they started doing something quite rash, and the Atlanteans who had places to go, went. They did not leave as from a sinking ship, they did not escape just to escape. They knew that they had to carry on. They had to go to places like Egypt, where they built the pyramids. They knew a lot of the biggest books they had would be destroyed. When people try to destroy the older prophets, they also destroy all their material so they will not be a threat to the new ruler or witch doctor. So they destroy not only the man with the knowledge, but all of the things that he has that they do not understand, that they cannot make work. If they cannot make them work, they fear someone else may come along who can. What they do not know, rather than try to learn, they destroy.

The Atlanteans knew this was coming, and knew they had a mission to save the important things in life, to be found and opened up at some future time in order to save the world. They spread out. The others stayed in Atlantis, to help when it sunk, or to try to convince the young ones that what they were doing was extremely dangerous. They went down with Atlantis when it blew up. The skies were red in the whole world for four days. Some of the land disappeared, and other lands were raised, and other lands buried. This always happens with the changing of the poles, and with what they were working on. But the knowledge was brought out. The knowledge was there and the knowledge was spread. The Indians and the Chinese accepted it, along with some of the very gentle white people. I call them white because they come from where it snows, but they are not really white. Some were white, some were brown, some of all different colors. I am calling them the colder people. Some of them went with a gentleness in their heart, with the knowledge in their heart, and were able to talk to both sides of the veil.

D: In the beginning, all language was one, all writing was one. People started changing the writing to suit themselves.

The man who wrote the beginning of the Bible in Hebrew just about started the Hebrew alphabet. He wrote it in his own shorthand, leaving out the a's and the e's, so that priests would understand what was going on, but not the common people. That was the beginning of the initiates.

The Chinese changed their language when they started putting it down in a shorthand of pictures. Other people used different alphabets. Some wrote backwards. All of the alphabets that have come down to you are shorthand. It has nothing to do with the original alphabet at all.

Moses wrote the beginning of the book you call the Bible. Moses started the Hebrew religion also, the Jewish religion. He came from the slaves. The Jews were not a tribe, they were a nation. They were people drawn from different nations, and used as slaves. Their slavery wasn't all that bad, not quite what you had here with the blacks. They were allowed to have their own houses and their own gods, and they were, at that time, pagans. Moses came down with the Christ Spirit within him, but there was an ego problem too, with our friend Moses. He did not know until many, many years later that he was of the slave people.

When Moses found out that his parents floated him down the river and the Pharaoh's daughter picked him up, that he was of the slave people, his ego problem was quite bad. First he wondered why his parents gave him away. (You have that nowadays with your adopted children. They want to find their parents. They have love and they have great anger.) Then he got angry that he was not of royal blood, because he could have been a Pharaoh. When people found out he was not of royal blood, no one would follow him, so he went off into the desert. He was a prophet, and like the instrument, a medium, and he sat there thinking about it. More and more he wanted to get even with the Pharaohs, and to show his parents they should not have given him up. I am giving you the human factor of the man Moses. The Christ factor of Moses did not come into view until he met the burning bush on the mountain.

Until then, he was quite human. He figured he had something very important to do, but did not know what it was.

When he came out of the desert and gathered up the people and talked to the Pharaoh, he had seen all of the seven plagues coming. He was also psychic. He thought, "This is the right time to get these people out of here. I will trade on this man's superstition. I know it is coming because I have seen, and I have great belief in the God that I saw in the mountain, the prophet or angel I saw in the burning bush." It was all the same thing, all psychic phenomena, so to speak.

Moses said to his brother, Aaron, "Let's give them something to believe in. I am angry at the Pharaoh, because I am royal and my people should not be slaves." Aaron agreed to go when Moses added, "You know if I talk to Pharaoh and the people, I am going to get so angry that I am going to want to choke them. So, Aaron, would you speak for me, and I'll tell you what to say?"

In the Bible, the seven plagues came down just as Moses saw it would, and he gathered his people and went into the desert. He had an unruly bunch of people. They were pagans. They had a religion, but it was idolatry, and this was not what Moses was looking for. He was looking for the unknown God, the God of all. So he went up into the mountains for about a month, and through meditation and prayer, he received the commandments for his people to live by. He did a lot of praying.

He was gone long enough for the people, who were without their so-called idols, to cast and make an idol of gold. Realize how long that took to first make a cast, to melt down the gold, to design it, to polish it. It could not have happened in a week, because these people were out in the desert gathering these things. They were of like mind: "You have given us nothing to follow except you, Moses. You have taken away our beliefs. You have taken away our idols. You have taken away everything and gone up into the mountain. You may be dead up there. We need something to believe in." The Bible will have you thinking that these people had no saving graces, that they didn't believe in God. But there was not God for them at this time. They had a God taken away, and Moses' God had not yet filled the void. They knew Moses believed in Him, and they saw a few things that looked like miracles to them, but over there they had a lot of miracles. A staff turning into a snake was easy for magicians over there. It was not a miracle to them. The parting of the sea was not really a miracle to them. The miracle was when it closed in and the Egyptians did not continue to follow them. They are pragmatic people who accepted and followed, and a lot of them didn't really see. (I know in the movies it looks so great and grand, but there were a lot of people following, and only the ones in the front really knew what was going on. The ones in the back weren't quite sure what was happening. They just followed.) They were people who needed a God. Moses knew if he took them into the desert and took away their God, and took away everything, he could replace it with his God. (This was much like your communists of today, except that in the communist countries, they have not yet filled the void. They think they have, but they have not. You must fill that void with something people can believe in.)

Moses went up into the mountain and meditated.

He came down with his tablets a month later and was angry, not so much that they didn't believe in his God, but that they didn't believe in him. They were saying, "Hey, Moses! You promised us a promised land. Look at what we've got! We've got absolutely *nothing*. We were better off as slaves. At least we had gold jewelry, and we could cook." Moses decided the best thing for him to do would be to write his story and teach these people about God. He sat down and it started coming through to him, much as spiritual writing and talk comes today. This is not automatic writing, but writing that comes by going into meditation, and recording the story of the beginning. He wrote it in his shorthand (which became Hebrew) so the people could not peek at it and understand it, or try to steer the others back to their pagan gods. He knew they wanted a story of creation to start with two, a man and a woman, and to go on from there. Otherwise, they would not believe him.

Aaron and Shem (I don't know if Shem was also in the Bible) were priests who believed in what Moses was doing. They were all messengers of God, touched by what you now call the Holy Spirit. They were all filled with the Christ Spirit. They knew these people, the Jews, could become a strong nation. (They did not stop to think that God never sent anyone to kill anyone in His name.) When people asked Moses the name of his God, he said, "It has no name." They wanted a name, so they called him Yahweh, but that is not the name of God. If you read the Bible, you will see that there are two or three different gods that Moses had to come up with for his people. One was a warring, avenging god, and he had to say, "God says this, and we must do it." And he had an all-forgiving god, which has a hint of the true God.

When you read the Bible, remember that all of the people in there were very human. This is what the Bible shows you: the story of their frailty, their goodness, and their evil. Some are very prim and proper, some are too good to be true, and some are almost too evil to be true. They are true men and true women that have been written about. The stories of all of these people in the Bible are true, but the hidden story, the moral behind this, is also there. You are not supposed to like everyone in the Bible. You are supposed to learn from them to do right, or to do wrong. You are not to judge them. You are to realize that each one of these people have the same frailties you have. I'm trying to show to you that you have taken Moses, David, and all these people and have made gods of them. You must realize they were human beings that all of you can emulate and be like. They all made mistakes, as you are allowed to make mistakes. They all had ego problems, as you have ego problems. They all were gentle and loving to different people. They were human. They were learning. They put on one shoe at a time like everyone else. What they want you to learn from the Bible is the mistakes that they made.

Moses did not get to the promised land because he killed a lot of people in God's name, not because he threw down the Commandments. If he had believed in God enough, they would not have had to fight and kill some very nice people. Of course they wrote that they were not nice people so that they could say, "This is the reason we killed them." Moses said, "Go ahead and kill them, and we will take over their land." Here in the Tucson area, if the transients started killing and taking over your homes and becoming so many that you didn't know what to do, you would be upset and fight back. This is what the tribes did against the Jews. Here was this horde of people coming through and saying, "Make way! Make way! God said this is ours." And you would look and say, "Well, God may have said this is yours, but I bought this land and I am living on it, and my children need to grow." But the Jews came and killed them and said, "This is the land that God gave to us." It was the land Moses gave to them, but it was not the land God gave to them. It was the land they took for themselves and said, "This is God's!" I am not blaming Moses. He did what was written, what he came down to do.

But I want you to look a little bit into the context of the Bible. By the time we get done with the Old Testament, when you do read the New Testament, you will be reading it a little differently. We hope you will be seeing it a little differently. We hope you will be seeing the fact that these are human people, writing human stories. It is a good book. It was one to follow, but not to follow too closely. This is why the Book of Miracles has come along and will eventually replace it. The people who read the Bible now take a part of it and almost jam it down your throat. Moses said this, Jesus said that, Mary did this, Martha did that. They might say, "It says here, 'An eye for an eye and a tooth for a tooth.' Therefore, I can take out your eye if you take out my eye." They have lost the whole context of the book which says: An eye for an eye, maybe, or a tooth for a tooth, maybe, but "I will do the vengeance," God said, not man on earth. They have taken that law and changed it. (I am thinking of Iran right now. My heart is a little heavy right now because of what is going on in my land. I know with people today, it is an everyday occurrence because of Iran and Iraq, but it is my land over there. Today is a very bad day for them over there, and I feel bad that there is nothing I can do to help.)

My main point is that everyone in the Bible, everyone, is a human being, and they all have their faults. When you find out that some of your heroes have feet of clay, please do not get upset, because we do not want to be revered. We want you to understand from our stories where not to make mistakes, or if you do make mistakes, that God forgives you, but you must forgive yourself. The Bible has become a book that has very little forgiveness in it, with what the religions are doing to it, and it is nothing but a book of forgiveness. It is laying out the stories saying, "Okay, I was an ass here. This is my story, and I was an ass. I was very arrogant." Or "I let them walk all over me." It is up to you to learn to do better. Many people today are not used to reading fables and understanding that each one has a moral. You can say to the people in the stories, "Hey, you were dumb!" or "Boy, you were clever!" It is to be read like a story, and the hidden meanings are within. Everyone asks, "Where can I find the hidden meanings?" because there is symbolism there. You can find it within your heart. You can read it. What does gold mean to you? What does silver mean to you? Look at a piece of gold. Look at a piece of silver. Get the feeling of it, positive or negative. How does it feel to you? The symbols are written on your heart. You have to look for them. You have to realize that the Bible is also a history of humanity. In perhaps forty or fifty years this book will be hidden away, and no one will be talking much about it. One hundred years at the most, and it will be dusty, hidden away somewhere. But the stories are so great.

We started slowly and surely with languages all one, writing all the same, but changed with people's shorthand or codes. This is how it changed, and Moses started the Hebrew written language with the secret writings.

Q: I am a little bit confused about the promised land. Did Moses fabricate the idea of a promised land, or was this just a military way of taking it? That seems to connect very much with the trouble we are having in the Middle East today, because there's the whole concept of the Holy Land.

D: The promised land that Moses saw was the same promised land that I saw on our side of the veil, not your side of the veil. The promised land is within. He, with his ego, and psychically seeing ahead that there was a place that they would stay because he was working out his karma, took these people and stole the land from the other people. Was it promised to God? No. The promised land that God promised is within. Moses externalized it to be without. In his travels he had seen this place and wanted it for his people, and decided to take it whichever way he could, in God's name. Moses was much like Khomeini is, and much like the Jews. They are of the same fabric. The ego gets in the way and they decide, "If I can do anything with God's help, I can do what I want here and not what I know to be. I have the power." And he had the power. He made these people into a fighting people.

Q: It's incredible to me that what was started there three thousand years ago is the same battle over the same issues today.

D: Yes. The more things change, the more things stay the same. India is the same place that it has been for thousands of years. People believe that they cannot help someone because they got the message wrong in the beginning. If someone over there has a broken leg, others will not help, because it is that man's karma to have a broken leg. They do not realize that it may be their karma to help that man. Do you see what I'm saying? They are stuck in a time warp, of going back until they finally learn that the promised land is within, and that no one kills for God, any God, no matter what name they put on them. Mohammed's God, Buddha's God, Khomeini's God, the Muslim God, the Hindu God. No God asks you to kill another person in their name. Stand up and say you are doing it because you want to do it, and you will have learned something. If you say, "God made me do it," or, "This is what God wants," you have learned nothing. My land is stuck in not learning anything. They are arguing yet. They had been for thousands of years, and then the Christians got into the act with their crusades and started the whole thing again. Whatever a religion or a sect calls itself, they are hiding behind the fact that they want power. The most powerful thing on the earth plane is God, and if I can make people believe in my God, I can do whatever I want, whether that is to kill or get money or become a king or high priest.

Q: You said that Moses began writing down the stories of Noah, Abraham, and Joseph, which were all part of an oral tradition. Was Abraham the father of the race, in a sense?

D: In a sense. Abraham was the father of the Jewish nation according to the stories told and brought down and spoken at campfires. A lot of it was lost, a lot of the other fathers. It was somebody's grand-father who started up a tribe, and as his tribe increased, this is the story that went down to their tribe. Remember that the tribe Abraham was the grandfather of intermarried with other tribes. He would leave and go to his wife's tribe in those days. Then he would bring that story to the tribe and they would meld it together. When Moses got hold of the story, Abraham was the father of the race.

Q: Where did Abraham get the idea that he had to sacrifice Isaac? Why the need to sacrifice?

D: I will tell you this much. People have always felt that they are what they eat. Now as people got to the fifth world, it changed to a feeling that if they are what they eat, if a brave man comes to me and I kill him and eat his heart or his brain, this will make me as smart as he is. If I kill an animal that is swift, it will make me swift if I eat it all, or if I eat the leg or parts of it. Therefore, if you had a child that you thought was great and smart, if you sacrificed this child, then God would become smarter because you were doing it in God's name, the same as you have eaten the hearts and livers of people and animals. They assumed that because they did it, God would want the same thing.

Q: Did the descendents of Joseph become the slaves in Egypt?

D: Yes, and they carried the stories with them. Remember, no one really started to write these down until Moses. He started pulling all this material together from the different people in the tribe of slaves he brought to freedom. He was a great historian. He wanted to pull it all together and make them one complete tribe, so he connected the thread within, and made it go from one to the other, perhaps changing a name here or there.

Q: So it wasn't so much historical fact as it was to create that common sense of history and destiny?

D: Yes, and to give his people something to pull them together and make them one, because each one had stories that were handed down from tribe to tribe. Bring it together, pull it together, and say, "This is what makes you a nation! This is what makes you God's chosen people." And yet the history is there, and each one could say, "Ah! I see. This is from my tribe. And you have it in your tribe? Then we must be one tribe. We must be related back to the beginning." He had people going around from tent to tent writing down the stories. (You do this today with your tape recorders. You go around to the primitive people and have them tell their stories before they are lost.) He wrote it down and compiled it, each family unit for a while. Some of them were large families units, some were small. While traveling, some heard the stories and said, "Yes! It is familiar. We are written about here. Joseph comes with many coats. I have heard about that." The many coats means the many tribes. The coat of many colors, the many tribes. Some of them even knew what colors the coat had and what color represented their tribe.

Remember, Moses was educated, and a lot of the people that he took out of Egypt were not. Moses made the book for them, and told them that this is what they need to know so that they can know everything. This brought the hunger within these people; the written word is so important that even today, they read everything and study, so that no one could keep them from learning again. Some, of course, did not want to learn. They were quite happy until Moses came along and showed them where they were discontented. Do you understand? They were not that unhappy being slaves.

Q: They came from many different tribes and Moses was creating a real unification, but it certainly wasn't very long before they were split back down into twelve different tribes again.

D: Yes, it is still the story of humanity. Though we are all one, or at least an earth of human beings, some people cannot get along with their own children, or the neighbors next door because they are a different color, or they speak with an accent.

All countries, although they seem to be one, are divided. Look at Ireland. Each faction is fighting for God, but for God knows what. It is an excuse. Each thinks if they say, "God does this," that he can do anything he pleases in God's name. Do it in your own name! Take credit for it, but then see how many people will follow you.

All your religious leaders on television say they are inspired, that only they speak to God. Everyone speaks to God. When your leaders come along and say to you, "I speak to God," you begin to think, "Perhaps I am not worthy to speak to God. This man speaks to God. God does not speak to me. I must do what he says." You're listening to yourself and God hasn't told you anything. Therefore, this person must know, and you feel inferior. Each one must speak for themselves.

Q: Was Moses any sort of an initiate in the pyramids? Was he trained in that type of power?

D: Yes, very definitely. There were Atlanteans all over who had intermingled with the people. When

he saw the burning bush, or the Holy Spirit, he remembered another lifetime when he was a priest,
and in the other lifetime his land was where he was
bringing the Jews.

Q: He had been in the promised land in another
lifetime?

D: Yes, and that is where he was heading, because
when he was there in another lifetime it was beautiful and almost empty. But that was maybe a hundred
years before, or two hundred years, and when he got
there it was a bit crowded. So he told everybody to
get out of the way, "We are coming through! This is
my land. I was here before."

❧

Everything went along until Moses found that his
people were persecuted. And he found what he
thought was a God, his God, everyone's God. But
he, of course, brought a new name for Him and got
his people out of bondage. You all know the story.
The priests from Egypt studied the antiquities, and
all knew how to do magic and many other things.
Moses also knew these things, because he went to
their schools as a priest in Egypt. It hurt him im-
mensely to see his people as slaves, and he brought
them out by his magic, by being a little better than
the others' magic.

Then he started writing the Bible, and he used the
religion of all people to write the Bible. The Bible
covers every book of every religion. They are parallel. They all have Adam amd Eve, or at least they all
have a paradise and a male and a female and a God
who creates. It goes along almost exactly with the
others, because he was writing from what he knew,

from the beginning, in a story for everyone to understand. His people could not read or write well, because slaves were not allowed to read or write well. He had to take the smarter ones and have them teach the others.

Moses came down with the Ten Commandments to hold his people together in the wilderness. If you read the Ten Commandments, they are perfectly logical to hold everyone together. None of them are hard. "Thou shalt not commit adultery." How great. Could you imagine trekking through the wilderness and having people squabbling over their spouse sleeping with that one and this one. Where would they get, yes? The same with "Thou shalt not steal." They went through a lot, even with the Ten Commandments, because many people paid no attention to it. There were always problems. Every week Moses had to counsel people, he had to be the deciding factor. He loved his people, but he got mighty fed up with all these little things. Their eyes should have been on God, on the future. But instead, they said, "Can I survive? Why can't I eat this? Why can't I do that? He's got more than I do." He finally found a place for them to go when he could not take any more, and they went there. Now he says he was sent by God.

I want you to remember one thing. God never told anyone to kill anybody in His name, ever. People were killed because other people wanted to kill them, not because God said so. God created all people, all souls, all spirits. He loves all people, all souls, all spirits. He would not have one of His children kill the other. If He wanted to kill someone, He would send down a volcano, thunderstorms, lightning, and tornadoes. He would not need one nation to go against the other, in God's name. Anytime anybody killed in God's name, it was sacrilege, because God does not kill one of His children, nor the other. He loves all His creations. All of them inside Himself, and outside. He could no sooner tell one of His children to kill the other than you could cut off your right hand for no reason. All of the killings the Bible calls God-directed were man-directed. Man did it, because man wanted to find a place to live, make a profit, or get rid of someone they were not happy with. Do not blame it on God. It is where it belongs, on man.

I killed because I had something to gain, because I was human, and I killed in God's name because people would believe me. It is easy to say God sent me. I did not do it in God's name. I did it because I wanted to do it, and I take the blame for it, yes, fully the blame. God asks no one ever to hurt anyone else in His name.

He sent Christs down many times to tell people to live together gently, love one another, be kind to one another. And each one of the Christs He sent down were gentle. They healed. They did not ask, are you Catholic, are you Protestant, are you Jewish, are you this, are you that. They saw someone who was sick and they healed. They could not stand pain in someone else, they would rather have the pain themselves. They were gentle, beautiful, loving people who came to ease the pain and correct what man has done to their teachings. Man has twisted it in his own way, shape, and form. Man has always done this, and perhaps always will, or at least for the next few generations, as far as we can see.

You must love one another. You look not upon what they are, who they are, what they do, what they've done: you do not judge. You heal and you love, whether it is a tree or a monster. Whether it is the murderer who kills a lot of people, or it is a beautiful little kitten. Every human being who takes another human being's life, or makes someone else miserable, does so only because they are miserable inside themselves, because they are sick, because they have anger and they must be forgiven, and they must be prayed for. You may dislike what they do, and what they do to others. I am not saying you must condone what they do. You can dislike that, but look at the tortured spirit that is doing it, and send prayers for them, so that in another lifetime they will not be tortured that way. You cannot judge anyone, ever. You can dislike what they do, but you cannot say that they will go to hell, because there is no such place, or that when they come back, they will have a lot to repay. *You don't know.* All you can say is, "They've hurt me and I feel angry. I do not like what they are doing. I will avoid them." You do not have to be near them. But pray for their spirit, not for the body that is going through that. You pray for the spirit. You send them blessings so they learn in this life, and do not have to be tortured in their next life when they come back.

None of you here are tortured souls, yet. You have been in other lives. This lifetime you have come through, and you do not have the bitterness. You do not have the bitterness, the anger, you are not tortured. You are blessed because you can now all see, or most of you. You are all more aware now than you were back in all different levels. Some of you are jumping up to higher levels. Some of you are staying. Some of you are walking and meandering, but you are getting there. But think back to what it could have been in past lives, when you were tortured, when you were angry, when you did kill. Forgive yourself, and in doing that, you will forgive the others. You will realize that eventually you have worked up to where you are now, with prayer, with help, with power, with knowledge, with knowing, with seeking. This is what you pray they find—or direct your energies to them, so that they will enlighten at some time. It does not mean now. It may not even be in the next lifetime. It will eventually. It eventually will get there and will help.

I do not believe in punishment. We cannot blame God when we hurt someone. We blame only ourselves. We do not hurt someone in God's name. God did not make you do it. The devil did not make you do it. You did it on your own. You've got to take responsibility for what you do. If someone attacks you, you react with instinct, in any way that you are supposed to.

It is not a sin to kill someone, because it doesn't actually make any difference whether you kill someone or not. It doesn't make any difference on your soul. It doesn't make any difference on your spirit. It doesn't make any difference to the world. You are just sending them into another state. You are destroying the vessel. You are not destroying their souls. You're not destroying their spirit. So it makes no difference. It is part of what is written, and you do it. It is how you feel about it that makes the difference. If you feel sorrow, if you are upset over it, then it makes a difference to you, not to the person you killed. It makes no difference to them at all. They are dead, or their body is destroyed, and they go back to our side of the veil where they belong, where true life is. They leave the play on earth and come to our side of the veil. They come home. Therefore, it does not make any difference to them. It may frighten them and they may have some fear in the next lifetime, or they may not.

What I am trying to say is, you can't blame someone else for your actions. You are responsible for all your actions. You are responsible for how you react to someone else. You cannot blame God for it, as most people do. Now, I am not saying that you are to carry around the guilt with you, for when you do something wrong, you realize that you did it. You did it, and that's it. You go on from there. Carrying guilt around with you is a very bad thing to do. You know you've made a mistake. You look back on it, and see if it changes your life.

Q: Is it a mistake if it was written?

D: No! But if you carry the guilt with you, then it is your fault and only your fault. You feel sorrow, or you feel righteous, if the person you killed needed killing. There are so many reasons to kill people. Say someone was killing everyone in the neighborhood, and you just happened to get off a shot and you stopped him. You would feel upset because you killed another human being vessel, but you would be pleased that at least you stopped him from killing more, you see?

Q: It's not a sin to kill someone?

D: I said it does not make any difference. It is not a sin against the person you killed. It is not a sin against God. It is a sin only against yourself, *if it is a sin*. It is according to who you kill, how you kill, and why you kill. If you kill in fighting, if you kill in war, can it be as much of a sin as if you've murdered someone? If you kill someone accidently, is it a sin? No. It is not a sin against them. It is not a sin against

God. It is perhaps a sin against yourself. They tried to murder Hitler. Would that have been a sin? Against whom? It would have stopped him from hurting other people, but would it have been a sin? We cannot judge, on your side of the veil, who has committed a sin against themselves, and who has not.

You have to look at the reasons. You have to look at the karma behind the act. You have to see if murdering or killing someone is not paying back a karma to them, or helping to release them from a karma. We cannot say what is a sin that you will die for, your soul will die for, your spirit will die for, you will go to hell for. A sin is supposedly against God. How can you possibly hurt God? That is ridiculous. He is beyond being hurt. He merely watches. You cannot hurt Him. The only ones you hurt are yourselves. Now, if you get angry, someone pushes you to killing them because they are coming after you, or they have driven you to the point where you just have to kill them, is that sin? Is that something that you have to feel guilty and angry and upset with yourself for the rest of your life? Is it something you have to go through, anguish and despair over, because you have taken another man's life, whether or not he deserved it? That is something that the spirit has to reconcile within itself.

The important thing with killing someone is the lessons you learn from it, and the lessons that the one killed learns from it. Not whether a human body is gone or destroyed, because human bodies are destroyed every day. You cannot hurt someone's soul, and you cannot hurt someone's spirit, as simply as just killing them. It takes longer—torturing them and killing them. There are so many variances here. There are so many things that you can bring in,

more than just killing someone, running over someone with a car, fighting someone in battle, or dropping bombs on people. You cannot live with that all
your life as a cross to bear. You must look at it,
rationalize it, try to change your life with it, so that
perhaps you may never do it again. Or perhaps you
stop other people. Use it either for the good or for
the bad; but know this, only you yourself are to
blame for anything you do. You cannot say someone
else drove you to it. You can merely say you allowed
them to drive you to it. You cannot blame another
for your actions.

Q: Are there killings going on in the world that
were not written beforehand?

D: No.

Q: I was wondering if anybody took off on their
own and did any killing besides what was written?

D: No, for you see you would not like to kill
someone unless there was a reason behind it. Even
the ones who go out and take pot shots at this one,
and that one, helter skelter, and do not even supposedly know them, are doing so. In New York City,
if it is your time to die, some way you will die.

You know the circumstances of killing someone in
war, it's kill or be killed. You feel sorry that you had
to do it, but not guilty. If you hate your parents and
sneak up and kill them, again perhaps guilt, but perhaps they drove you to it. You cannot judge whether
they are guilty or innocent. You do have to have law
and order. You do have to have people decide what to
do with someone who is outside of society, but in
that case you are judging the body. You are taking
the body out of circulation. You are putting the body
into prison. You are electrocuting the body. It is the
body that you are hurting. You are not hurting the

soul. When you judge, you are judging the body, you are not judging the soul.

When you say, "Oh, the man next door doesn't clean his house properly," or "She doesn't take care of her kids properly," that's judging. You don't know that he should clean his house. You don't know whether she is taking care of her children properly or not. Just because she is not doing what you do, or he's not doing what you do, it does not mean that they are wrong. That is putting your judgement on them. You're judging their soul. You are judging them as people. *You do not judge someone else*. If you do not like what they do, you do not have to go over there and see them. But you cannot judge because you do not know what they are doing is wrong. It is written that they do it this way, therefore this is the way they should do it.

Each one is an individual. Each one has their own soul, their own spirit. Each one is at a different level than the other. Each one is working on a different karma than the other. You cannot make everyone be like you. You cannot have everyone act the way you act. In this world called earth that you are on, everyone should go their own way. Everyone has a right to be themselves. Everyone has a right to flower the way they wish, as long as it does not go against the laws. Now, if the man next door has his place so dirty that you can smell it from your place, or it is a dangerous firetrap, then you have a right to call someone, or to go over and help him. But, you must not judge him to say he is wrong, because that is the way he lives comfortably and enjoys. You may go over and help him, explain to him that the odor is bothering you, or you are afraid your house will catch fire, and come to a friendly agreement, if possible. But other than that, you have no right to judge. If the man next door gets up at six o'clock in the morning and mows his lawn, don't sit there and scream at him inside. Get up and say to him, "Please, could you wait until seven or eight because I am trying to sleep." But do not say, "Oh, he does not like me. He gets up every morning at six o'clock and mows his lawn because he does not like me." You do not know until you have gone over and spoken to the man nicely. If you go over in anger, then you will get anger back.

What you give out, you will get back. You cannot blame anyone else but yourself for it. If you give out anger, you get back anger, maybe not today, maybe not until thirty years from now, but you get it back. If you give out love and peace and smiles, you may not get it back right away, because of the anger that you have sent out before, but you will eventually. Try to send out peace and love. And to send out peace and love, you must feel peace and love inside of you. You must not feel slighted by what someone else says. They do not mean it. And if they do, it is their problem. You only get angry and hurt if you allow them to hurt you or make you angry. Have you ever tried to start an argument with someone who just sits there and smiles at you and says, "You're right, you're right." You cannot, because they will not rise to the bait.

We decided, since pre–Atlantean times, since the beginning of this world, that we were going to write out our stories. We write out almost to the letter what is going to happen, hoping that eventually we will bring some semblance of order to the chaos in our lives. It may take many thousands of years, maybe many millions of years. It took us seven, eight million years to get into the situation we are in, and it may take us that long to undo it. You know it is not time. It is always now, so time doesn't mean anything. If you look back to the beginning, we believe it was billions of years ago, but we are not mathematicians. They will find out that the earth is a lot older than they give it credit for, and man has been around since the beginning. If you realize we have been around since the very beginning, how many years are in just five million years. Think how many lifetimes you have been here. Maybe you were here two or three million times.

What do the other worlds mean? They were here. They have been destroyed. What has come forward from the other worlds is the knowledge that *God is*. We are within God, and we have the power. Our minds are still as powerful as they were before. Our minds are as powerful as that of the man Jesus. Jesus' mind was powerful. All we have to do is to atone or attune with God, know that we are of God. We are part of God. What God can do, we can do. God's mind is our mind. We can do it if we want to.

What holds us back is our fear of getting the power again and misusing it. For all of you here had the power and have misused it. Of course you felt sorry, and are now afraid to open up for fear that you will get power-hungry. It frightens you to open up and use it, which is good, because this time you will not do it in a hurry. You will get it slowly and be able to use it when you get it. In the beginning when we first had it, after a while it became a toy, to see who could do this and who could do that. Now it is not a toy.

Now it is an at-onement. Now we will use our powers for the good of mankind. We will realize that fire burns, and we should use it properly. We will go on from there, ever building our lives, ever building love. In the beginning, I said if I could write a book of a thousand pages about religion, I would put just one word on each page: LOVE. That is what it is all about. Love yourself and love others. Love this chair, love the birds, feel an at-onement with them. Allow love to come into your hearts and minds, and you are on the same wavelength as God. The powers that you have will get stronger.

Your healing powers will get stronger, for if you love someone enough, you will use the energy from God and heal, without even thinking. Some of the healers today say, "I will heal this one and I will heal that one. I know this one. I feel sorry for them. I will try to heal them." Yet they will pass by people on the street who are not well. Jesus passed by no one. Some people are selective of who they heal, or who they pray for. They do not try to heal their enemies, and they do not try to heal people they dislike, and that is most important. Your enemies should be healed first, for in doing so, you heal yourself. People you dislike should be healed first, because in doing so, you heal yourself.

Of course, as I said, Moses' God was Moses' God. There are a few different Gods in the Bible. Moses decided that the people needed to feel at one with something, and he found the way to that. He felt at one with, and he created or named him Jehovah, Yahweh, the One. If you read the Bible, you will see there are many Gods; some are gentle, some are angry.

Men use God to fit the situation, but no one used God more than the Christians. They made God angry, terrible, fearsome, vengeful; zap, and you disappear. God does not get angry. God does not make people disappear. God allows you to do as you want, but he does not say you must do this. Why should He? He created you just like Him, with the same intelligence, with the same mind. You are a part of Him, and if you are a part of Him, you think like Him. Just like a piece of the ocean has all the properties of the whole ocean. You are a part of God. He does not have to tell you what to do. You do not sin. There is no hell. There is no devil. The Christians invented it. Jesus did not invent it. The Christians invented it, and the Jews do not go along with it. The Buddhists do not go along with it. Only the Christians, and they try to get everyone under their thumb by saying, "Yes, you will go to hell if you do not do as we say." It is a period you have to go through.

For five million years, we have had no hell, we have had no devil. These last two thousand years we have a hell and a devil. Always something new under the sun. Nothing is ever new under the sun. What is the devil? Misguided spirits, misguided people. The priests have always tried to get the people under their thumb with some sort of terror. The Incas did it. They sacrificed people way back, even to my time, even to the beginning. Cain and Abel, yes, the beginning. So the devil is not new, they just have given it a new name. Hell you provide for yourself on either side of the veil. If you want to have a hell on my side of the veil, you can have it, we do not stop you. But we are trying to tell you it is not there, it is only in your mind.

We are all important. Every spirit is important, no matter from where. Jesus said the least of us are important. That goes for the spirit of the animals. The flowers, the fairies, and man. Man always thinks he is the smartest because his mind works. The animals' minds work, the brownies, the fairies, their minds work. No one has ever asked their opinion. No one has ever thought they had an opinion, because in the Bible it says, "Man has dominion over the animals." That means he gets to take care of the animals, that he can become one with the animals, not that he is better than the animals. If he were better than the animals, he would not have to kill, to steal clothes and shelter, to make bombs. The animals do not have to do this. They live at-onement with God. Who is smarter? Many people have said, "Oh, my dog is so smart. Maybe someday he will be a human being. Poor little thing." Poor little thing! The poor little thing does not wish to be a human being. He has not worked himself up and does not wish to. He is where he is and perfectly happy being an animal soul, an animal spirit on this planet. On other planets, who knows. Perhaps they are a higher intelligence form than man.

 ❧

Q: Were sacrifices to God an idea of man?

D: Yes.

Q: God never asked for them?

D: God never asked anyone to kill anything, person, place, or thing.

Q: I always wondered why he wanted all that burning, fat, smell, and so forth.

D: Yes, it does not interest him at all. Man tries to make God happy by giving back to him the best.

Q: Then God doesn't really want it?

D: Why would He want it? He creates it. If he wants it, it is His. The whole world is His. He cre-

ated everything. He is everything. He owns everything. Why would He want one of His beautiful
creations destroyed in His name? Would you want
your most beautiful daughter or son destroyed in
your name because you made it? No! Would you
want one of your precious animals destroyed in your
name because you created it?

Nothing was ever destroyed in God's name, that
He ever asked for. And I am saying "He," Mother-
Father-God, the One. It is not a he. It is all. It is
balance. But never does He want anything destroyed
for His sake. Man has said, "If the Gods look with
favor upon me, I will throw the virgin into the
volcano, and it will stop the volcano." The volcano
was stopped only because it was going to stop, if it
stopped. Every time a volcano belched, somebody
was sacrificing something into it. Especially the
priest, and the ones he sacrificed were usually the
head man's daughter, or someone who would not
give in to him, or someone that he could take something important from. It comes down to avarice,
to greed, that is why the priests had them thrown
into the volcanoes. A good way to get rid of your
enemies.

In Hawaii, the Polynesians banged their enemies
on the head, dug a hole, and made the four cor-
nerstones with the bodies buried underneath, so that
their spirits would guide and guard them. The
spirits haunted them, because no one likes being
knocked on the head and buried in sand as a cor-
nerstone. They haunted for a while and it did keep
other spirits out. It frightened everyone to death, except the man who was inside, because he got rid of
his enemies and he was strong enough not to feel the
spirits. *The spirits can only hurt you if you are afraid of*

them. There are no bad spirits. There are no good spirits. There are mischievous spirits. Some have a sense of humor, some like to frighten, but they cannot hurt you unless you allow your imagination to go along with it, and allow them to do so.

We walk in God's temple. We are within God. Everything is within God. Everything is blessed. Everything is holy, and everything is sacred. If one person touches it, it does not make it more holy than someone else. If you put your energies into it and your energies are stronger than someone else's, then it can help. Your energies can make something strong or weak. But that does not make it holy. Again, it is not in God's name. It is in the name of the person who does the blessing, every time someone blesses someone. The Catholic church goes around with the holy water and blesses. All of God's water is holy. Everything in the earth is blessed. One man cannot make it more so than another.

God does not have favorites. God loves all. God gets too much blame. We use God as a torch, you know, I am on God's side, therefore God is on my side, nonsense. God is always on your side. God is on everyone's side. God loves all. He loves everything that has ever been made or created, good or bad.

You love your children. You made them, someone made them, yes? You get angry at them, but do you condemn them? You love them. No matter what they do, you love them. You may walk away from them, but you still love them. God loves all. He is on no one's side. He is on everyone's side. His power is there to be used.

Do not feel because God is behind you that you are better than anyone else, or you have more answers than anyone else. It is because you are attuned to the energies, you are attuned to the healing powers, you are attuned with the laws, the universal laws of nature that you can make things work for you. Now I am not saying do not believe in "God." God is there, God created, this is His temple, everything should be respected. Everything should be loved, but do not use God as an excuse for anything, against someone else. God loves the man who has killed people. He loves the people in the crazy house. He loves those misbegotten children that are misshapen and deformed. He loves all with the same power. All He requests is that you love one another as He loves you, and that is how you prove your love for God.

You do not prove your love for God by saying, "God, I love you, God, I love you." He knows that. But when you prove your love for Him by helping someone else, by loving someone else, another one of His creations, then you prove to God that you love him. Thank Him by being nice to someone else. Thank Him by doing something for someone you do not like, and then you truly thank Him. As Jesus said in the Bible, when you give water to someone in need, you are giving water to God.

Q: Does God expect us to prove our love for him?

D: No, but people want to go around proving they love God, and they go to their churches, and they give lip service to God, they give lip service to their religion. They say they want to be spiritual. They tell everybody, and in the meantime, they kick dogs and cats. They will not be nice to their in-laws. They beat their children, and do these things, and say, "I love God. God, I love you, I love you." That means absolutely nothing. You prove love, you prove caring by doing. What I am trying to say is, by lip service you prove nothing, by actions you prove everything. And some people do feel the need to prove not to God, but to their friends, to their relatives, to everyone that they love God and that they are spiritual and holy. Do not try to prove it, do it.

Q: I wanted to ask you about Babel. You said after that Babel humans wrote up their lives. What happened at the Tower of Babel?

D: At Babel, there was confusion. The Tower of Babel means mass confusion. If you know the story in the Bible, it says that everyone got together and tried to build a tower all the way up to God, and they all spoke the same language. After a while there was great confusion, and they were sent to different sections. I use Babel as a symbol of mass confusion that was going on, even before that.

We on this side decided it was easier to write out our own stories, to remember our own karma, our own cause and effect, our own reincarnations, and to aim toward going back to the spiritual side of God. In the beginning we kept trying to straighten it out here. Then came cause and effect. There has always been cause and effect in nature, but we did not realize that we could make the plan on our side first, and then work it out down there. That way we are lightening up our karma. We are doing what we are supposed to do, and we will get everything out, back into harmony, for the end times, whenever that comes, which is quite a way off.

Q: You speak of respecting the body and caring for it and so on, and yet, the various means of death in human life are so horrible that it makes one wonder if the body is so sacred. How can it be treated the way it is from time to time?

D: Your temple is holy to you. It is in your care as long as you are alive. You are to take as good care of it as you can, but not extraordinary care, because it wears out. It is like a vessel that will decay eventually. It is not a permanent thing. You change it as you change a dress or a pair of pants. When you get a new pair of pants you take extra care of them, is that not so? But then as they start getting old, you start taking less care of them, because they are starting to wear out. You do not have the right to abuse your own body, without perhaps damaging your spirit and your soul. People do bring on their own psychosomatic diseases. They should learn not to, not only for their body, but also for what the imprint of the aches and pains do to the spirit and to the soul. But you are three in one, and must be treated as one, so by learning to stop psychosomatic illnesses, you are learning to stop punishing yourself, your body, your soul, and your spirit. Start forgiving yourself, and start going in the right direction for yourself in beauty. It does not mean that some people are not to die from cancer, for it is written in. A body is sacred only as long as it is alive and is doing the job that is written. You should try to take care of it. It is a gift, but gifts wear out, bodies wear out.

Q: Some cities tend to have more murders than other cities. Are we then to assume that spirits with that kind of karma would gravitate to those areas?

D: You have just about answered your own question. People always gravitate to where they are supposed to be. They are called there, as the Jews were in Germany. Sometimes it is the karma of the place to attract people like that. New York City, since inception by the European countries, has been a place of a lot of murders, a lot of killing, a lot of discontent. Before that, there's little known, but the Indians did little on the island and were very happy to sell it, because they did not like the feeling of it. They did not have any villages on it. Look back into it. They didn't have to get rid of the Indians on Manhattan Island, because the Indians felt it was a place of taboo. Things were not happy there, and the Indians would have gladly put up a village there if it were a nice place. They know by energies where to bring their villages for good. They tried never to bring for evil. They were happy to give it to the white man, for his own evil. And so you will see with many of the places where the white men live, or the Europeans.

Where there is calm and peace, you will find cities of calm and peace, and people who are peaceful and calm will go there. Much will happen because of the energies. There are many of them, places of power. Most of the religious places have much energy, much power, much beauty.

Q: So the geographic location has negative vibrations that attract the people, rather than the people coming and creating the negative vibrations there?

D: The people should eventually learn to offset the negative vibrations and bring joy to it. It can happen. You can move into a house that has negative vibrations and change the vibrations by being positive. But people who go to these places are negative anyway and do not wish to change. It is like a magnet, it draws, but there are people trying to change it, there always have been.

Q: Can a few people do it, or would it take many to change the vibrations of an entire city?

D: It would be according to the size of the city, for there are good people in some cities, but there are not quite enough yet.

Q: We realize that all of our spirits lived many years, many times. Are we then to assume that any murder that occurs now is not for this particular spirit?

D: Yes and no, for you have to learn to murder someone, and learn to be murdered so that you will know, inside of you, how it feels to be both, and to have pity for both.

Q: Once you are murdered, it seems as though the cycle has started and you tend to murder who murdered you.

D: But then it is over.

Q: Can it happen that one be murdered and then get to the point where he does not want to murder again?

D: It can happen, and perhaps it does happen. But if you wish to pay it back, it will happen by accident, by dropping something out of a window in New York City, or running over someone in a car by accident. Again it would be against your feelings. You would feel very bad about it, it is an accident as far as you're concerned, but still it is killing someone. It is over. There are so many nuances in just living, so every life, every human being, every spirit is an entirely different story. It is difficult for us to make any generalizations.

This is why we say you cannot judge. You can deal only with yourself, and then not too harshly, for when you come to our side of the veil you judge yourself. If someone says, "Oh, I am stupid," they are judging themselves harshly. Or someone says, "I

am good." How do you know? You are talking yourself into it. You are judging yourself and doing the
action that you are upset with yourself about. Say
merely, "I have done this thing that is wrong. If I
could change it, I would. I am sorry. I will now try
to lead a life that will not allow me to do the same
thing again." If you notice, I said, "I will try to." You
cannot say I will, because if you falter, you will lose
faith in yourself. All you can do about your past
mistakes, whether it is killing someone or losing
your temper, no matter how nasty you have been, is
realize it and wish to change, and forgive yourself.
Then you are on the upward path. If you are nasty
and you do not want to change, then it will not
bother you anyway. Only the good people, the ones
who care, have guilt, and they are the ones we are
trying to reach to tell them, "Do not have guilt, but
go onward from there. Forgive yourself and try to do
good for others and for yourself. Do not stay in the
same place blaming yourself in despair."

Q: If you have to kill somebody in your lifetime,
do you tend to do it before you start on your spiritual path upward, or are there spiritual people who
wind up killing because it's been written?

D: Look at Jim Jones. All those people who died in
Guyana were not bad, some were children. It was
written. It was written so people would notice. It
was written, just as Germany was written, just as
Biafra was written, so people would notice what is
going on. So people will not become too involved in
cults, following and making a god of a man. You see
how they made a God of Jones? He said "Kill yourselves," and they did. There are many people in this
world who make gods of people. People are not
gods with a capital "g." They are gods with a small

"g," and each one is a god. But do not make a god of a human being, for you can affect him and harm him even more than you can affect and harm yourself. That is what happened to Mr. Jones. They sent out the energy that they thought he was God, and he absorbed it, and thought he was God. So it is not his fault alone. It is the fault of all of them. I am excluding the children, but of course again it was written that they would go with their parents.

Q: So nobody is really exempt at any stage?

D: No, no one is exempt from living. This is what it is all about. No one is exempt from despairing, and no one is exempt from saying, "I do not believe there is a God. I believe God is a devil. I hate God." At times human beings are pushed to where they say that. What I am trying to say is, do not blame God for your mistakes, or where you have led yourself.

Q: I was wondering about the power you said we all once had and lost. Is this the energy that we're building up with our chakras now?

D: Yes, but every human being on earth has the same power.

Other human beings who are not into the spiritual path are using it for other things. I am not saying for wrong things, for good too, for creation. In this generation, people on earth are becoming more used to the power. We are allowing it, bit by bit, to come in so that we all may learn how to use it properly this time.

Q: When we're ready for this power that we've written ourselves to come, does it automatically come? I have heard of people who suddenly knew things that they'd never known before, and I wondered if this was part of that power.

D: It is for them. You will have to wait and see.

Again it is how much you give yourself, how afraid you are of using it, how many times in past lives you have been on the verge of using it, how much you will allow yourself to get. Everyone has the same power, every spirit, every human being. All they have to do is know how to channel it the way they want, for good or for evil, and then go to the limit. Some people do not know how to control their power and some do. There are as many different levels of power as people in the world. I mean the power of the mind to do what it wants, to move things if it wants. But be careful you do not use it for tricks or just to prove you can do it.

I would suggest that if you want to use this power, if you want to get it, you use it for someone else and not for yourself. Use your healing power for someone else and not yourself. If you truly do it for someone else, in doing it for them, you heal yourself. If you use it merely on yourself, it will not work, because your spirit knows you are being selfish with this power. And if you are on a spiritual path for your own gains, it will not be good to have power just to prove you have it. Enough power will be given to you for the needs you have and the needs you wish to fulfill. Whether it be more of one or less of the other means absolutely nothing, because you have what you can deal with on your own, what you need for you. Do not waste the power on tricks. Use it for good, for that is what it is for. You bring in karma again, cause and effect, retribution. If you use it for tricks, then in the next lifetime you may want it badly and not have it. Cause and effect. It is the rule of the world, or the worlds, it is the law of the universe. Anything you do comes back to you, at some time or another. It may wait four thousand years to come back, but it comes back, because you owe it. It is cause and effect; you send it out, you must get it back. You see people who live nothing but good lives, yet are plagued with so many things, and you wonder why. Maybe four thousand years ago they did something and are not in the balance yet, and it comes back to them.

Q: What do you mean by the balance?

D: Karma, cause and effect. They caused something to happen four thousand years ago and it comes back to them. They did something bad and it comes back now. The scales of justice, cause and effect. You take from here and this goes up. You must take from here to put here, to balance. Good, bad, you do so much bad, it comes back to you. You do so much good, it comes back to you. But do not expect that, because you do so much good in one lifetime, that only good comes back to you in that lifetime. Because of the law of karma, you have to make up for past lives. It is the way it is, my friend. It is how you take it this time and deal with it, that either wipes it out for good, or if it makes you bitter, then you start it again.

Q: All the spirits seem to be on the path of evolution toward perfection. Is there the possibility of making a mistake and stepping down, and starting all over again, or are we on a continuous upward cycle toward perfection?

D: I would not say continuous upward cycle, because there are some lives where you go down a little. But you do not fall all the way back to the bottom. You just go two steps backward, and do it over again. But if in the next lifetime then, you do it again, then you go another two steps back. It is up to you, but eventually it works out, for deep in our

spirits, this is the path all people on earth are following. You may look at your earth now and say,
"You've got to be kidding. There are a lot of people
here who are not following any path." You do not
know what they are working out in this lifetime, so
that in the next lifetime, they can come back and be
more spiritual.

Q: Who decides what time you leave earth?

D: You, your spirit, not your live body or your
soul or your will, but your consciousness. Your consciousness says this is it.

Q: If you do something to somebody else, then it's
going to come back to you. Does it come back to
you ten-fold?

D: Let me put it this way, it will seem ten-fold.
You may steal a nickel from somebody who is rich
and can afford to lose it. But when it is stolen from
you, it may be the last thing you have between you
and destitution and starvation. It is ten-fold and still
a nickel.

Q: When we say it has been written out, does it
mean that a group of us wrote it together?

D: Yes. You get together much as the actors in a
play. You figure out what the play is going to be, you
pick out the actors for the roles by mutual consent,
and you say, "In this I would like to do this. Could
you possibly do this for me?" You do not have a
writer who is doing the whole thing. You are the
writers who come to the agreement that this is the
way the play will be written.

Q: In a way, if somebody hurts you in this lifetime, you can meditate very deeply and realize that
you had agreed that person was going to hurt you?

D: Yes, because you have hurt them, in another
lifetime that you don't even remember. It may be a

complete stranger. Someone you do not know comes along and beats you. But this is someone that in another lifetime you beat. You learn from the pain. You forgive your enemies. If you can get over it by being grateful to them because you have learned a lesson, it ends the karma like that. If it bothers you and eats at you, the karma is not over, and must continue again. Cause and effect. You are hating them, you are starting the karma. Cause and effect. You hate them, in another lifetime, they will hate you. Simple, but so difficult.

Q: So when we're in the spiritual world, we don't have much feeling toward the material when we set up all these scenes for ourselves, and then we have to come into the material world and live with what we wrote up?

D: Think of it as a play. Each actor has a part, and each actor brings to it what they want. Living drama, that is all it is, and it does not last as long as you think it does. It seems like four hundred years to you until it is time to die, and then you realize, "Oh, my lord, I've only been here for seventy-nine years. It is not enough time. I want to stay."

Q: Is there an audience?

D: There is always an audience, because no one is ever alone. In the room now, we are not here alone. You each have your guides, the dogs have guides, and other people who sit in this room just because they like the feeling. The instrument has her guides, her friends who are on the other side, people passing through. I tell you my friends, if only you could see how crowded this room really is. Everyone learns. That is what earth is. It is a school of learning, a crash course, a school.

Q: Is what you are teaching going against the

teachings of Julian? [Julian is the entity which channeled through another medium and gave Jeanette
Kandl her first exposure to channeling.]

D: I am going in a slightly different direction. He,
of course, is teaching positive thinking. Positive
thinking works, but it does not work for everyone.
You must realize that we are not teachers, but guides.
We give you a message. The ones who are to hear,
who have it written in this lifetime to hear, will hear.
It is as if we give them a key to open a door. We are
reaching the people who are ready to open that door.
It will not work for everyone. Julian is saying to his
groups that for them, if they want to use it, it will
work. Mine is going out in a book to the masses.
The power of positive thinking was in a book to the
masses. If everyone could use positive thinking, they
would be using it now, and one would not negate the
other. Say for instance that a woman had a boyfriend
she positively thought was going to marry her. Another woman positively thought he was going to
marry her. Both are using positive thinking. If he
married one of them, the other would have to lose
out, even with her positive thinking. Does it mean
that the one who positively thinks harder will win?
No. It means that the one who it is written he will
marry, will marry with the positive thinking.

This is guidance. We are guiding for the initiates,
for the ones who say, "Oh yes, I know this is for
me." It works. But if it worked for everyone, the
world would be in a worse mess than it is, for people
would use positive thinking as wrongly as we did
our powers. If it were that simple, some would use
positive thinking for evil and some for good, and
again you would be in the same battle ground. Remember this: in some teachings, someone will hear

something and say, "Oh, this is fantastic. I will use it." That is, for that week. The next week, they will hear another teaching and say, "Oh, that is fantastic, I will use it." Three or four weeks later, you ask them what the first teaching was and they have forgotten it. It is good only for the moment. They do not work on it. We are trying to tell the people that positive thinking works if it is supposed to work, if you work at it, if it is for the right reason. But you cannot go around positively thinking, "I am going to have a steak dinner tonight," if you've only got two cents in your pocket. You positively have to say, "If I want a steak dinner, I am going to positively make the money to pay for it." Or perhaps a friend will call you up and take you out. That is entirely different. Positive thinking is not for those who think it great for the first week or two and then forget about it, for of course it does not work instantly. It is a rule to live by constantly. It is something that has to be worked on and perfected and believed in. You believe in it, you use it for the rest of your life, and when it works, it will work right. When it does not work, it is because it is not in your best interest for this to happen.

Q: Many books today tell people how they can use their inner powers to do things like bring them large amounts of money. Are there any pitfalls in doing this, and in what way must it be repaid?

D: The only one who is truly making money on that deal is of course the author of the books. They have positively thought that the selling of the book will bring them a lot of money, but they have worked by making a book to get the money. You have to work for what you get in this or any lifetime. It is again karma. What you get easily, you lose easily. Again, you are working with the power of positive thinking, for good or for evil. It is not evil to wish for a lot of money and to get it. You must earn what you get. If what you get back is bad for you, it is because you earned that bad in other lifetimes or in this lifetime. If what you get back is good, it is because you earned that good in this or other lifetimes. Now I am not saying that people who take a chance and win a million dollars did not put effort into it. They did. They took a chance. The chance was that, this time, they were to win the million dollars. This was written in for them, and it is good for them, perhaps. Now let us see what they do with their money, whether it is good or bad that they got it.

Q: Does the expression, "It is written," that you've been using a lot, mean that all of us have destiny we have to follow? If it is so, can we ever change that destiny, through free will?

D: Destiny of course means unchanging. What you change is your feelings as you go through it. You will go through it. If you go through it with acceptance and joy, saying, "This is a lesson I have to learn, I will not be bitter about it," you will change your next lifetime, your next destiny. You will erase karma. If you go through it angry and upset, and that feeling comes back with you to this side of the veil, then you must work it out. If you can work it out on earth so that you end up accepting and not bitter, you erase karma that way. But changing the destiny of this life is difficult. The important thing is to know what it is, and remember it was written before you were born.

On our side of the veil, there is no time. The past, the present, and the future are one. I cannot give you all of the simple answers. We give answers, but we are not allowed to give you every answer you need to know on earth, for we would be cheating. You would not be taking the tests properly. Our answers are merely to guide you until you get to those tests. Much like a teacher would say to a nervous student, when you get to this part, you know what the answers are. Sit there and write them all out, and do not get upset over it. This is merely what we can do, for living on earth, the answers come from within you. We guide you to expect this or that in life, so that when it hits you, perhaps it doesn't hit you quite as hard, or you know how to deal with life. But we cannot tell you what is going to happen to you; if you knew everything that you are supposed to know about this lifetime, it would be a wasted lifetime, for you would not learn. You would learn only as much as a student does who steals the test answers and cheats. They learn nothing, just as you would learn nothing in this lifetime.

We are here merely to guide you, to help you over the rough spots, to give you something to think about when you read this book. When you listen to what I am saying, you will say, "It is written, but I do not know what is written. I must pass each test." Suppose you were an English teacher. A student comes to you and says, "I can't find out what Shakespeare said here and here," and you say it is written, go and research it. If they are having a difficult time, you will say, it is in this book, it is in this play, go and search it out. If they are still having difficulty with it, you will tell them it is on page so and so, and from there they must do the reading themselves. You cannot give answers to what life is. We cannot give answers to what life is about. We cannot give instant cures, for that would not help anyone. You must go through every test; all we can do is give you the courage to face your tests, the courage to go on, the knowing that we are here to help you, the understanding of telling you to look into other people's souls before you judge them.

We tell you not to judge. Do not say, "They are doing this to me." Take the blame on yourself. "I am allowing them to do it to me. Why am I doing this?" The blame goes to no one. It is always with yourself. You must look inside, find out why you are allowing someone to upset you. Maybe it is from a past lifetime, something about them that you dislike, or something about them that is much like you, that you resent. You see the negative side of you in people you resent. Something within you allows this to happen, and either you reconcile this or you walk away from the situation. For in truth, it may be that they see something in you that they do not like, or they have a past lifetime with you that they remember with hate. That is their problem. Pray for them and walk away from them. Do what you can to resolve it inside, and when you walk away, do not walk away with bitterness or hate. Walk away with love. Walk away saying, "I love you. This is your problem. I will not add to your problems by being around, but I will pray for you so that you may work out your problems. I have to work out mine."

When you love someone and try to help them out with their problems, you have to stand aside from yourself, unemotional, and try to help them with their problem. If you help them with an emotional tie, it will block the true answers from yourself. We are trying to teach you to be slightly unemotional, not in your relationships with people, but in dealing with people and problems. You cannot carry someone else's problem with you all day long, worry about it, or work it out for them. You get upset over it and it bothers you. But then, you forget it emotionally, and eventually the answer will come to you clearly. Emotions are in the way of what to do and how to help them. As long as you are emotionally involved, you do not think clearly. We are trying to get you to leave emotionalism out of tight situations, and put it into situations where people need love. You can love people and not be emotionally upset over things that happen to them, that is the best way. You can be upset and you can care, but when your emotions start getting involved, you pull down the shade and cannot find an answer. We are not being cold by saying this. You have to stand back from emotions, even when it has to do with yourself. Stand back as an outsider and say, "If this happens, am I making too much of it, or too little of it? Am I blocking it? Am I not knowing? Am I not understanding something or someone else? Am I understanding too much?"

Everything you have to deal with may be a personal crisis. I would suggest that you write it down, almost as a math problem, clinically and coldly, and try to figure it out. You put the pros on one side and the cons on the other. Write down what decisions you could make, from every which way, and figure it out almost as if it does not belong to you.

Or, the best way, of course, is to let go and let God. Go to sleep and know (positive thinking), know that the answer will come to you and that you will accept it. Though the answer may not always be what you want it to be. Some people want an answer from God, or from their higher entities, or from someone, but the answer that they want is the one that they want, and they want to hear no others. There is a quotation: "God works in strange ways, his wonders to perform." What we have to do is pray for the strength to go along with the understanding that God has, your guides have, your higher self has, go along with them and know they are right. Eventually you will see, "Oh, of course, I did not get a purple one, but green is just as good." Or, "I did not get the answer I wanted, but the answer that came is better than I demanded." And demand is what most people do when they pray to God. They say, "Dear God, I want the answer to this, and I want the answer to be what I want." Now sometimes, as a test, God will say, "Then we will give it to you just the way you want it," and sometimes that is the worst thing that you have ever gotten. But when you pester enough and want enough, you get it, and find out that it is definitely the wrong thing.

Suppose someone wanted a red Cadillac, even though it got only five or six miles to the gallon, and wanted it very badly. And God said, "You may have it, but you are not listening when I am showing you compacts. You can have it." So they get it, but now gas is impossible to get. Now they want to sell their car that they prayed so hard for and would not listen to the true answer. They have it, and they cannot sell it. Nobody else wants it. They've not paid it off yet. They can't get gas, and have problems that will get worse. But they got their car. They got what they demanded from God.

Be careful what you demand from God. It is always best to say, "Dear God, these are my needs. Help me to fulfill them. If they do not seem like needs to you, then give me my needs, and let the luxuries come in if I deserve them." It is like having a birthday party and telling each one who comes to your party that you want this gift or that gift, and having none of them show up, or having a birthday party where you ask for nothing and they bring you riches.

I have tried to cover from the beginning until this lifetime. I am not going to explain this lifetime in this book. I am trying to give a clearer understanding of who and what you were, before you became what you are today. You have been many things, many people, and on different planets. You have been spiritual, you have been evil, you have all looked for the balance. You are all in this lifetime accomplishing the balance. In this lifetime, you are making up for some of the bad karma that you have sent out, or the vibration that is coming back. As I have said to you before, your karma comes back to you ten-fold. But at times, if you work hard enough in a lifetime, it does not seem ten-fold when it comes back to you because you can deal with it, and it is not the crisis that it seemed to be. I said that if you stole a nickel from a millionaire, in the next lifetime he may steal your very last nickel, and you would feel it ten times more. But if you are optimistic about it and say, "Well, it is better being broke than the way I am," and accept it, then nothing would come to you, because you are not building the karma back with anger. You are erasing it, and allowing good vibrations to come to you. So then it does not seem ten-fold. If you take it as a joke and say, "C'est la vie," someone may come along and offer you a meal so you do not starve. But if you get angry, maybe someone will not offer you a meal, and you will starve. What you do with your spirit is in your hands.

It is not always in your hands what you do with

your body. You are to take as good care of your body as you can, without taking extraordinary care, for even it wears out. Even if it is maimed or sick, it is still your body. Some people look at their bodies with disgust and hate. You cannot hate your bodies. It is what you chose to come back in. It is your vessel, whether it is deformed, sick, or ugly, it is still a gift from God.

Some people wear beautiful dresses, and if something happens to a dress, they give it away. Then other people wear the dress until it starts wearing out, and perhaps they give it away. Someone down the ladder gets this worn dress, and they repair it and repair it until it falls apart. That is like your body. The ones with the beautiful dresses are the ones who have the beautiful bodies. The ones who have the next one are the ones who have bodies not so beautiful. The ones that repair it and try to take good care of it are the ones with the broken bodies. But they still appreciate it, and should still love it, because it is covering and holding your bones and your soul and your spirit together.

It is a gift and gifts should never be laughed at or looked down upon, for gifts are usually given with love. If they are laughed at or looked down upon, in another lifetime, when you give gifts, they will be laughed at and looked down upon. Accept all things gratefully. If you cannot use them, give them to someone who can. But do not laugh, for you are laughing at the love that was given behind it, the thoughtfulness, and you are laughing at a living thing. Even a dress contains atoms, and is quite proud of whatever it looks like.

Handle all things gently. This cane has been cut from a tree for fifty-seven years. It is still alive. It still has atoms, it is still proud that it can help man. It is not dead, it is very much alive. It has been put in a closet. It has been hung in a cellar, it has not been used but it stood there waiting, knowing that some-day, someone would rescue it and it would be useful. Everything, even this rug, is doing its service. It is old and dirty, but it is alive, and it cares. If it is handled with care, it will give back love and good vibrations. If you say, "Oh, it's old, it's dirty, it's not good. I don't like it," it will fall apart very quickly, for it hurts and it feels.

Everything should be handled gently. Your bodies, your toys, the earth, the dirt, the sun, the moon, everything that is within God, as we are all within God, should be handled gently. The food you eat should be thanked for growing and dying for you, to help you grow, so you may die and grow. If you eat and do not appreciate the food, it will not agree with you. It may make you fat, it may make you sick, it may make you break out, or become constipated. Accept it as a gift, as a gift of that thing, that leaf, that meat. If you thank the trees, or the oil, or what-ever has made your clothes, they will not wear out so quickly. They will stay. They will be appreciated. Everything is within God and a part of God. We are within God and a part of God. He is within us, but He is within and without. He saturates. He is, we are.

The ones who are truly enlightened can expect to grow and be spiritual, and they will grow and be spiritual. The ones who say there is heaven and hell and no one can go farther, will not want to see any-one going farther. If they die with that embedded in them, they will, of course, still be prejudiced when they get to our side of the veil. It takes a lot of growing. Do not think that because someone dies they suddenly become much smarter on our side of the veil. If they have not been able to use their intelligence on earth, if they have been stubborn and opinionated, then they will be stubborn and opinionated where we are. They must slowly absorb what we are teaching, and let the veil lift from their eyes and see what outside the veil is truly like.

On your side of the veil, you tend to make gods and goddesses of people who are along the path. This is not good for them and it is not good for you. Accept them as humans with a beautiful gift. And gifts are not always used. Do not be upset with them. Just love them for having a spiritual fight. Being spiritual is almost harder than being truly human, for when people look up to you, you have to try to live up to that, and sometimes it gets to be a bit much. You just cannot live up to their expectations of you, and when you fail, or just a bit, they think you have gone twenty steps down instead of just making a half step down. So be gentle with your friends who are spiritual. Be gentle with your friends that you do not understand. Be gentle with your friends who are your enemies. My sermon today, my friends, is to be gentle and love, for if you love, you are truly gentle.

Q: Do you see us?

D: Yes, I see your auras. I do not see exactly what you look like. I see auras.

Q: Is it you who keeps the medium's eyes closed?

D: Yes. If we opened them, she would come back. She is very curious. To us, because we have not been in a body for many of your earth years, on this incarnation it is very easy, because opening up the eyes is hard to do. Keeping them closed is very simple.

Q: David, do you use anybody else as an instrument to come through?

D: On the earth plane? No, but that does not mean that I do not help others to find answers.

Q: Could you use someone else?

D: If it was prewritten, yes. Now there are a lot of people who say they have David coming through them, a lot of people who say they have Jesus coming through them. It is the name that comes along. It is not the same person, though they may work in the same school, so to speak. No, on the earth plane, in the Americas, I am working with Jeanette. In other countries, I am a helper with other people in other churches, or other meetings, or other schools. It's just a group of us getting together and helping in different places.

Q: Can John the Baptist, or a counterfeit, come through to individuals?

D: I am coming through, am I not? But there are a lot of John the Baptists, there are a lot of Davids, there are a lot of Jesus', there are a lot of Virgin Marys. We come through on a signal that people want to hear. If someone wants to hear that John the Baptist is coming through, and will believe what he is saying and listen to it, and perhaps open spiritually, someone called John the Baptist will come through.

Q: Would it be the essence of that individual?

D: Sometimes it is not even the one you think it is. It would be another John who baptized.

Q: The reason for the difference is different energies?

D: Yes, and the ego of the instrument that it comes through. They would not accept that I'm Daisy Mae. They want someone else, John the Baptist or Jesus. For us, it is just a telephone number that you are calling and we are answering, and we have to teach to the group. We cannot teach above them to where they will not understand. We cannot go to someone who enjoys hunting animals and teach them they cannot shoot anything, and preach that to them. They would get angry and leave. They want to hear that it is all right to hunt. We have to teach what they want to hear and slide in things of awakening to them. You have to get their interest.

Q: Is it possible for anyone to channel from any of the levels?

D: Yes.

Q: Are we able to bring in the highest energies from the highest levels?

D: You can if the people you are channeling for will understand and accept the higher levels.

Q: If not, does someone else come through?

D: Yes, but when you say *lower* levels, you are thinking of good and evil. Each person you channel through, or the person who is channeling, chooses to help the multitudes. You can't talk to someone who is only in kindergarten at a college level. So what will come through you is kindergarten stuff for the kindergartners. Whether the entity you are channeling is higher or not depends on whether someone who is philosophical would want to teach kindergarten. But we are on tap to help any one of them at any time, with any question that comes up.

Q: What about the stronger or heavier vibrations? In some of the channelings they said they wanted to raise my vibrations to the point where I could channel x, y, or z, so that I would be able to handle the higher vibrations. I feel the difference in the energies.

D: You see, we could not completely jump into your body without lining you up because we would burn you out in seconds, so we have to try to meld together. We have to try to either lighten or increase our vibrations as you either lighten or increase yours, so we do not do a lot of damage. But, may I tell you this, with each one of these there is damage to the human body.

Q: In what connection?

D: For every hour we use up at least two, maybe three, hours of your energy on the earth plane. The energy drain brings stress onto the body. That is why someone could not go around in a trance constantly, because they would burn up. We do not do that. We have to line up and do as little damage to your nervous system as we can, for the vibration rate is very different, and try as we can, we cannot just go like a snap of the fingers and not worry about it.

Q: Is channeling the same as a deep trance?

D: It is a lighter energy, but we do use your energies. There is a drain of energy, yes.

Q: Does the spirit then help to replenish that energy, or to help that body?

D: We try, but there are many variables, like whether the instrument wants to accept, or whether we zap them with too much energy, too much of a healing. You realize we are not around 365 days of your year to figure our such adjustments. We would be interfering with your lives. Each one of us, as each one of you, has a different energy, different vibrations.

Q: Why is it that you like to hold something in your hands?

D: As a king, and as a shepherd, the crook or the staff were never far from my hands. It is something I enjoy holding when I come into an earth body, because it grounds me onto the earth and reminds me where I am. Some are more used to being in the body. I have not had the privilege of being here very often, so this reminds me that I am here and to stay until it is over. It is a grounding force.